PRESIDENTS

Melissa Blackwell Burke

Publications International, Ltd.

Melissa Blackwell Burke is a freelance writer of a variety of educational materials for both student and teacher use. A former elementary school teacher, she also writes children's literature and has published both fiction and nonfiction books. She is proud to live in Texas—the birthplace of two presidents and the home state of three presidents—with her husband and daughter.

Consultant **Laurie Winn Carlson, M.A., Ph.D.,** has written 20 nonfiction books. Carlson teaches history at Eastern Washington University.

Illustrations: Drew-Brook-Cormack Associates; Map Illustrations: Susan Carlson

Picture credits: **AP Images**: 9, 13, 16, 40, 44, 46, 49, 54, 57, 61, 63, 65, 67, 69, 70, 71, 72, 73, 74, 75, 76, 77, 82, 85, 93, 95; NASA, 76; Cecil Stoughton, White House, 79; U.S. Air Force, 73; U.S. Navy, 88; Vermont Historical Society, 67; **Archive Photos: 25; Art Resource**: National Portrait Gallery, Smithsonian Institution, 20, 26, 28, 32, 34, 36, 40, 44, 46, 47, 50, 52, 54, 58, 60, 64, 66, 68, 70, 72, 76, 80, 84, 86, 88, 90; Printed by permission of the Norman Rockwell Family Agency Copyright © 2002 the Norman Rockwell Family Entities, 80; Réunion des Musées Nationaux, 12, 20; Smithsonian American Art Museum, Washington, 17; **Ash Lawn - Highland, Home of James Monroe, Charlotteville, VA**: 19; **President Benjamin Harrison Home**: 26, 54; **Calvin Coolidge Memorial Foundation, Inc.:** 67; **The Carter Center**: 85; © **Corbis**: cover, 35, 36, 37, 38, 39, 41, 42, 45, 50, 51, 57, 61, 69, 92; AFP, 92; Bettmann, 11, 13, 18, 20, 23, 24, 25, 26, 33, 35, 38, 42, 43, 49, 53, 55, 56, 61, 63, 65, 68, 69, 83; Joyce N. Boghosian/White House, 94; Michael Christopher Brown, 95; David J. & Janice L. Frent Collection, 37, 43; **Dwight D. Eisenhower Library:** contents, 75; **FOLIO, Inc.:** 8; Ted Hooper, 15; Jon Riley, 73; **George Bush Presidential Library**: 88, 89; **Courtesy Gerald R. Ford Library**: 83; **Getty Images:** AFP, 95; Archive Photos, 17; FPG International, 41; Hulton Archive, 23, Newsmakers, contents, 93; Arnie Sachs/CNP/Hulton Archive, 90; Telegraph Colour Library/FPG International, 87; **Globe Photos**: 45, 58, 59, 65, 66, 70, 71, 82; NBC, 77; Dave Parker/Alpha London, 89; **Gilbert Gonzalez/Hayes Presidential Center**: 46, 47; **Courtesy of HarpWeek, LLC:** 43, 50; **Harris - Ewing News Pictures:** 23; **Harry S. Truman Library:** 73; **Herbert Hoover Library:** 69; **The Hermitage, Home of Andrew Jackson, Nashville, TN:** contents, 22, 23; **The Image Works:** 41, 59; B. Daemmrich, 76, 92; Sonda Dawes, 91; Richard Ellis, 90; Keystone, 89; Nicholas Lisi/Syracuse Newspapers, 93; Larry Mangino, 91; NASA, 81; Mark Reinstein, 87, 90; Topham, 63, 64, 71, 72, 79; David Wells, 86; **International Stock:** Chuck Mason, 84, Ryan Williams, 85; **James K. Polk Memorial Association, Columbia, TN:** cover, 31; **Courtesy Jimmy Carter Library:** 9, 84, 85; **Collection of the Kentucky Museum, Western Kentucky University:** 32; **Library of Congress:** 12, 17, 21, 25, 27, 29, 33, 44, 52, 54, 55, 63; **Lyndon Baines Johnson Library:** 79; Mike Geissinger, 79; Yoichi R. Okamoto, 78; Cecil Stoughton, 78; Frank Wolfe, 79; **Used by permission of The McKinley Museum, Canton, Ohio:** 57; **The Metropolitan Museum of Art, Gift of I.N. Phelps Stokes, Edward S. Hawes, Alice Mary Hawes, Marion Augusta Hawes, 1937:** (37.14.34), 21; **Minnesota Historical Society:** 67; **National Archives:** 69; **Collection of The New-York Historical Society:** 62; **Nixon Presidential Materials Staff:** contents, 81; **Ohio Historical Society:** 64, 65; **Peter Newark's American Pictures:** 33, 48, 53; **President Benjamin Harrison Home:** 26, 54; **Ronald Reagan Library:** 87; **Science and Society Picture Library:** 47; **Cecil Stoughton, White House/John F. Kennedy Library:** 8, 77; **Shutterstock:** cover; **SuperStock:** cover, contents, 4, 6, 7, 9, 10, 14, 15, 16, 21, 25, 28, 31, 36, 41, 53, 59, 60, 76, 87, 90; City Art Museum of St. Louis, 34; Cummer Museum of Art and Gardens, Jacksonville, 22; David David Gallery, Philadelphia, 10; The Huntington Library, Art Collections, and Botanical Gardens, San Marino, 12, 14, 40; Jack Novak, 28, 72; Stock Montage, 11, 22; **Theodore Roosevelt Collection, Harvard College Library:** 58; **The Western Reserve Historical Society:** 49; **William Howard Taft National Historic Site:** 60; **Whitehouse.gov** 94

Poster credits: Art Resource: National Portrait Gallery, Smithsonian Institution; Réunion des Musées Nationaux; Corbis; Gilbert Gonzalez/Hayes Presidential Center; HultonArchive/Getty Images; President Benjamin Harrison Home; SuperStock: Cummer Museum of Art and Gardens, Jacksonville; David David Gallery, Philadelphia; The Huntington Library, Art Collections, and Botanical Gardens, San Marino; Jack Novak; Whitehouse.gov

Pictured on front cover, clockwise from top left: Abraham Lincoln, the Statue of Liberty, Barack Obama, Mount Rushmore, and George Washington. **Pictured on back cover, clockwise from top left:** Andrew Jackson, Zachary Taylor, John F. Kennedy, and a campaign banner for James K. Polk.

CONTENTS

A Look at the Presidents

Ever since George Washington took office, the American people have been curious about their presidents. In fact, Washington took trips across the country so that people could get to know him and he could get to know the people he was leading. Each president has his own stories about life before, during, and after the White House. And each president adds something to the nation's story.

- More presidents were born in Virginia than any other state. Eight presidents have a birthplace in the state called "Mother of Presidents." (Of course, when some were born in Virginia, it was actually still a part of England.) Ohio ranks second, with seven presidents born there.
- Thirty presidents graduated from college, and only nine presidents didn't attend college at all.
- Almost two-thirds of all the presidents served in the military.
- Twenty-six presidents studied law and became lawyers. More than half served in the U.S. Congress before becoming president. Seventeen served as governors of their home states.

Mount Rushmore is a symbol of the office of president of the United States. The faces of George Washington, Thomas Jefferson, Theodore Roosevelt, and Abraham Lincoln represent the growth of the nation in its first 150 years.

- At age 69, Ronald Reagan was the oldest president to take office. Theodore Roosevelt was the youngest, at age 42.
- William Henry Harrison, the ninth president, served the shortest term in office—only 32 days. He was the first to die in office. Franklin D. Roosevelt served the longest term. He was elected four times and spent 12 years as president before dying early in his fourth term. (In 1951, a change was made to the Constitution so no president may serve more than two terms.)
- Four presidents—John Quincy Adams, Rutherford B. Hayes, Benjamin Harrison, and George W. Bush—were elected without earning the most votes of the people. Adams was chosen by a controversial vote in the House of Representatives; the others were chosen based on the outcome of electoral college voting.
- Nine presidents did not serve out their terms—four died, four were killed, and one resigned. William Henry Harrison, Zachary Taylor, Warren G. Harding, and Franklin D. Roosevelt all died of natural causes while in office. Abraham Lincoln, James A. Garfield, William McKinley, and John F. Kennedy were assassinated. Richard M. Nixon resigned from office.
- John Tyler had the most children of any president. He was the father of 15. Three presidents, James Monroe, James Polk, and Andrew Jackson, had no children of their own.
- Two sons have followed their fathers to the White House. John Quincy Adams (6th president) was elected after his father, John Adams (2nd president), had served. George W. Bush (43rd president) followed his father, George H. W. Bush (41st president), into the White House.
- Most presidents worshipped at Protestant churches. John F. Kennedy was the only Catholic to be elected president. Three presidents said they followed no particular religion.

- Gerald Ford lived longer than any other president to date. Both he and Ronald Reagan reached the age of 93, surpassing John Adams's mark of 90 years. At age 46, John F. Kennedy was the youngest president to die.
- Herbert Hoover had the longest retirement of any president—31 years. James Polk had the shortest. He died just 103 days after he left the White House.
- Three presidents, John Adams, Thomas Jefferson, and James Monroe, died on the Fourth of July—our nation's Independence Day.
- Barack Obama was the first African American elected to the office of president. He was also born in Hawaii, making him the first president born outside the continental United States.

Birthplace Map

°States are correct, but place names often vary.

ARKANSAS
Bill Clinton
● *Hope*
CALIFORNIA
Richard M. Nixon
● *Yorba Linda*
CONNECTICUT
George W. Bush
● *New Haven*
GEORGIA
Jimmy Carter
● *Plains*
HAWAII
Barack Obama
● *Honolulu*
ILLINOIS
Ronald Reagan
● *Tampico*
IOWA
Herbert Hoover
● *West Branch*
KENTUCKY
Abraham Lincoln
● *Hardin County*

MASSACHUSETTS
John Adams
● *Quincy*
John Quincy Adams
● *Quincy*
John F. Kennedy
● *Brookline*
George H. W. Bush
● *Milton*
MISSOURI
Harry S. Truman
● *Lamar*
NEBRASKA
Gerald R. Ford
● *Omaha*
NEW HAMPSHIRE
Franklin Pierce
● *Hillsborough*
NEW JERSEY
Grover Cleveland
● *Caldwell*
NEW YORK
Martin Van Buren
● *Kinderhook*
Millard Fillmore
● *Locke*
Theodore Roosevelt
● *New York City*
Franklin D. Roosevelt
● *Hyde Park*

NORTH CAROLINA
Andrew Johnson
● *Raleigh*
James K. Polk
● *Pineville (Mecklenburg County)*
OHIO
Ulysses S. Grant
● *Point Pleasant*
Rutherford B. Hayes
● *Delaware*
James A. Garfield
● *Cuyahoga County*
Benjamin Harrison
● *North Bend*
William McKinley
● *Niles*
William Howard Taft
● *Cincinnati*
Warren G. Harding
● *Marion*
PENNSYLVANIA
James Buchanan
● *Mercersburg*
SOUTH CAROLINA
Andrew Jackson
● *Lancaster*

TEXAS
Dwight D. Eisenhower
● *Denison*
Lyndon B. Johnson
● (near) *Johnson City*
VERMONT
Chester A. Arthur
● *Fairfield*
Calvin Coolidge
● *Plymouth*
VIRGINIA
George Washington
● (east of) *Fredricksburg*
Thomas Jefferson
● *Shadwell (Albermarle County)*
James Madison
● *Port Conway (Orange County)*
James Monroe
● *Colonial Beach (Westermoreland County)*
William Henry Harrison
● *Charles City (Berkeiey Estate)*
John Tyler
● *Greenway*
Zachary Taylor
● *Gordonsville*
Woodrow Wilson
● *Staunton*

THE OFFICE OF PRESIDENT

The Founders carefully considered the office of president when they wrote the Constitution of the United States of America. This document clearly details who can become president, how the president is elected, and what a president does.

Any person who is born a citizen of the United States, is over the age of 35, and has lived in the United States for at least 14 years may become president.

In a presidential election, all U.S. citizens over the age of 18 can register to vote. On Election Day, the American people head to the polls and vote for their candidates. This is called the popular vote. The popular vote leads to the electoral college vote—the vote that decides the presidency. Each state has a set number of electoral college votes. This number is equal to the number of senators and representatives a state has in Congress. When people mark their ballots on election day, they are choosing their representation by the electoral college. Usually, the candidate winning the most votes in a state earns all the state's electoral votes. Representatives called electors cast the actual votes in the electoral college. Electors vote in December following a popular vote. Votes are officially counted in Congress in January. The candidate that receives the majority of the electoral vote—at least one more than half—wins the election. If no candidate gains a clear majority, Congress chooses a president from among the candidates who received the most votes.

The winning candidate takes the oath of office on January 20 for a four-year term. The president has many duties. One is serving as the Commander in Chief of the Armed Forces. Another is choosing judges and other officials, as well as representatives to work with other nations. Some of these appointments must be approved by the Senate. Thousands of other

I do solemnly swear (or affirm) that I will faithfully execute the office of President of the United States, and will, to the best of my ability, preserve, protect, and defend the Constitution of the United States.

With these words, a person officially takes the oath of office of president.

Today, American citizens 18 years and older can vote, no matter their race, creed, color, or gender. It wasn't always that way. African American men won the right to vote in 1870. Women were first allowed to vote in 1920.

Electoral College Map

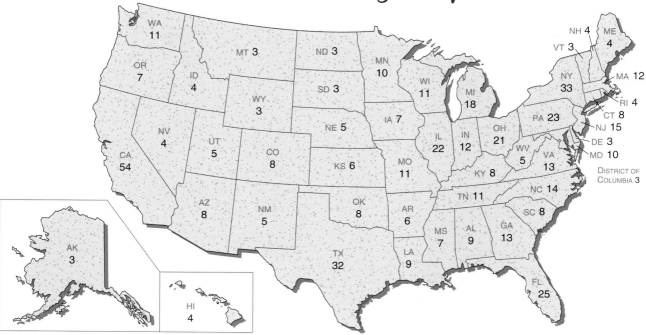

* *Numbers according to the 2000 U.S. Census.*

Before 1937, presidents were sworn in on March 4. Today, inaugurations (the ceremony in which a president takes the oath of office) take place at noon on January 20. Inaugurations have been times of great celebration in the country with receptions, balls, and parades.

mportant government posts are chosen by the president alone.

The president is the leader of his political party. The president suggests laws for Congress to consider, but Congress has to agree to them before the laws are passed. And the president has to agree to the laws before Congress can pass them. A president can prevent Congress from passing a law by using the presidential veto.

The president shares information with Congress in the State of the Union Address. In this message, the president describes the progress the government has made. It also details what else the president would like to do for the country.

The president is also in charge of relations with other countries. One of the powers the president has is to make treaties, or agreements, with other nations.

All in all, the president of the United States is the nation's Chief Executive Officer. The president must lead the nation and, in the words of the Constitution, "shall take care that the laws be faithfully executed."

THE PRESIDENT'S HOME

The president of the United States lives in a house owned by the American people. Today, it is called the White House, but it has also been called the President's Palace, the President's House, and the Executive Mansion. President Theodore Roosevelt made the name the "White House" official in 1901.

This landmark was built more than 200 years ago. Every president except George Washington has called this building home. The house was designed to serve as the president's private home, as well as his office. Although George Washington never lived there, he took part in choosing the site and the design of the home. John Adams was the first president to live in the house. It was not quite finished when Adams moved in near the end of his term.

The president works in the West Wing of the White House, in a special space called the Oval Office. The White House offers a tennis court, a jogging track, a swimming pool, a movie theater, and a bowling lane for when the president is not working.

The White House has 132 rooms, 8 staircases, and 3 elevators. It also has 412 doors, 147 windows, and 28 fireplaces. Right: *The Green Room.*

Scorch marks from the War of 1812 are still evident on this wall of the White House.

When the home's second resident, Thomas Jefferson, moved in, he made improvements to the home. Jefferson built wings onto the house that added office and storage space.

A few years later, the British set fire to the house during the War of 1812. The inside was completely destroyed. But the outside walls withstood the blaze. President Madison saw to it that the house was rebuilt to look exactly as it had before the attack. He wanted to send a message to the world that the building, and the new nation, would always stand strong.

Throughout the years, presidents have updated the mansion. They added running water, electricity, telephones, and porches. When Theodore Roosevelt took office, he decided that the president's offices needed to be more separate from the living quarters. He ordered construction on a new West Wing for office space. Since then, every president has conducted the nation's business from the famous Oval Office in the West Wing.

By the time President Harry Truman moved into the White House in 1948, the house was not in good condition. Years of visitors walking through and a series of minor building changes had weakened the structure. Truman ordered that the house be rebuilt to make it stronger and safer. Again, the outside walls were reused. Everything on the first and second floors was designed to look just as it had throughout history. Two basements were added. From the outside, though, the White House remained the same—a symbol of our nation's history.

The White House lawn is the site of many special events, including the annual Easter egg roll.

Today, the White House is a living museum. It is still the private home of the president and his family as well as the command center for the country. But it is also a place that people visit to see the beautiful furnishings, important artworks, and the site of much history. All tours are free of charge.

The First Families enjoy all that the White House has to offer. They can explore the President's Park— a huge yard filled with trees, gardens, and fountains. They can swim, play tennis, watch a movie, hit balls on the putting green, or go bowling at the White House lane. Mostly they can be a family living together, although their home is one of the most famous houses in the world.

GEORGE WASHINGTON

In 1789, George Washington did something no man had ever done before. He took the oath of office to become the president of the United States of America. Washington is called "The Father of Our Country."

George Washington was born in Virginia, which was then a colony of Britain. In time, people grew unhappy with Britain's rule. As an adult, Washington spoke out against Britain's unfairness. He organized an army to fight the British and was chosen to lead the troops. After six years of war, the British surrendered on October 19, 1781. Washington became a national hero.

Free from Britain, the 13 former colonies formed a government, but it had serious problems. Washington led a group to solve the problems. The group wrote the Constitution of the United States, which set up our present system of government. In the first presidential election, George Washington

1st President
Born: February 22, 1732
Died: December 14, 1799

Term of Office
1789 to 1797

Party
Federalist

Vice-president
John Adams

First Lady
Martha Dandridge Custis Washington

Washington was the only president who never lived in the White House. During Washington's presidency, the nation's capital was in New York City and then in Philadelphia. But Washington would have been content to stay at his family home, Mount Vernon (right), with his family. He had married Martha Dandridge Custis, a widow, who had two children Washington loved.

John Adams

John Adams helped shape our great nation and later became its president. Though he is remembered for his political ideas, he was not always a skillful politician. His term as president was important because it showed that the new country could change leaders successfully.

Adams was born on a farm in Massachusetts when it was a colony of England. He went to Harvard and excelled at the study of law. He believed strongly that the colonies should be free to make their own laws. Adams was a delegate to the First and Second Continental Congresses and was a leader in gaining independence from Great Britain. During the Revolutionary War, Adams worked with leaders of other countries in Europe. He helped create the peace treaty with England.

During the first presidential elections, the candidate with the most votes was elected president, and the runner-up was vice-president. John Adams served two terms as vice-president before winning the presidency. A proud and stubborn man, Adams found serving as vice-president difficult. He felt he had little to do. That changed when he became president.

During Adams's presidency, France was at war with England. This caused problems for the United States at sea. Adams did not want another war. He talked to

2nd President
Born: October 30, 1735
Died: July 4, 1826

Term of Office
1797 to 1801

Party
Federalist

Vice-president
Thomas Jefferson

First Lady
Abigail Smith Adams

Adams was the first president to live in the White House. When he moved in, during his last year as president, the house was not quite finished. Adams wrote to his wife, "Before I end my letter, I pray Heaven to bestow the best of Blessings on this House and all that shall hereafter inhabit it. May none but honest and wise Men ever rule under this roof."

the French, but they continued to battle with Britain. Finally, Adams got the French to agree to peace. Adams's political party was angry, though, since they had wanted war. Adams did not win reelection. He returned to his farm in Massachusetts. Adams died exactly 50 years after the Declaration of Independence, which he helped draft, was approved.

John Adams and his wife, Abigail, were married for 54 years. Because of Adams's posts overseas and in other states, the two were often apart. They wrote hundreds of letters to each other over the years, often focusing on political topics. Abigail Adams once urged her husband to "Remember the ladies. Be more generous and favorable to them than your ancestors."

When Adams sent leaders to discuss peace with France, the French demanded a bribe. The United States refused to pay. Adams reported this to Congress, but he identified the Frenchmen who asked for the money only as "X, Y, and Z." Adams and the nation were outraged by the request. This became known as the XYZ Affair.

John Adams was the first president to be the father of another president (the only other father and son are George H. W. Bush and George W. Bush). These two houses on a farm near Quincy, Massachusetts, are the birthplaces of John Adams and his son John Quincy Adams.

Adams had the government build new ships to establish a navy. He is sometimes called the "Father of the American Navy" for his efforts.

THOMAS JEFFERSON

Before Thomas Jefferson died, he wrote the words he wished to appear on his gravestone: "Here was buried Thomas Jefferson, author of the Declaration of Independence, of the Statute of Virginia for religious freedom, and father of the University of Virginia." Jefferson didn't list being president, but he was a great president. He is remembered for making sure that government stayed in the hands of the people and for expanding the country westward.

Jefferson was born into a well-to-do family in Virginia. He had an education that included many areas of study—several languages, mathematics, philosophy, and science.

Jefferson was a man of many talents: He was an architect, an inventor, and a musician. He became a lawyer and was elected to the Virginia legislature. Known as an excellent writer, Jefferson was asked to write the Declaration of Independence.

For the next 20 years, Jefferson served his country in different positions, including as governor of Virginia, U.S. minister to France, secretary of state for George Washington, and vice-president for John Adams. In 1800, Jefferson was elected president after months of electoral college voting to break a tie between him and Aaron Burr. As president, Jefferson arranged the Louisiana

3rd President
Born: April 13, 1743
Died: July 4, 1826

Term of Office
1801 to 1809

Party
Democratic-Republican

Vice-presidents
1st term: Aaron Burr
2nd term: George Clinton

Acting First Ladies
Dolley Madison (friend)
Martha Jefferson Randolph (daughter)

Jefferson had a library of more than 6,000 books. These became the start of a new Library of Congress. The Library's first collection of books had been destroyed during the War of 1812.

The Jefferson Memorial was dedicated in 1943 on the 200th anniversary of Jefferson's birth. The simple, classical architecture reflects a style Jefferson favored. A 19-foot bronze statue of Jefferson graces the center of the white marble monument. Quotes from Jefferson's writings appear on panels around the memorial.

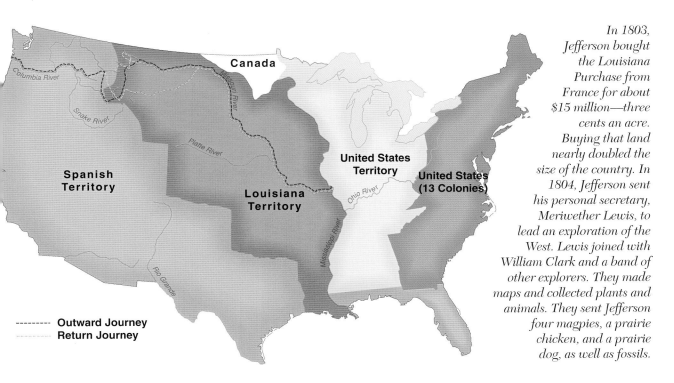

Canada

Columbia River
Snake River
Missouri River
Platte River
Spanish Territory
Louisiana Territory
Rio Grande
Mississippi River
Ohio River
United States Territory
United States (13 Colonies)

-------- Outward Journey
-------- Return Journey

In 1803, Jefferson bought the Louisiana Purchase from France for about $15 million—three cents an acre. Buying that land nearly doubled the size of the country. In 1804, Jefferson sent his personal secretary, Meriwether Lewis, to lead an exploration of the West. Lewis joined with William Clark and a band of other explorers. They made maps and collected plants and animals. They sent Jefferson four magpies, a prairie chicken, and a prairie dog, as well as fossils.

Purchase, in which he bought all of France's western lands. Jefferson was reelected in 1804, when, for the first time, electors voted separately for president and vice-president.

After his second term, Thomas Jefferson retired to Monticello. For the next 17 years he stayed busy making improvements to his home and setting up the University of Virginia. Thomas Jefferson died on July 4, 1826—50 years to the day after the Declaration of Independence was approved. It was the same day his friend John Adams died.

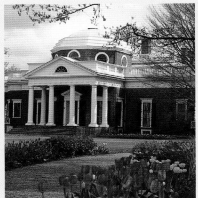

Jefferson loved the home he designed. Monticello is perched on a hilltop in Charlottesville, Virginia, and its name means "little mountain." The home has many special features planned by Jefferson, such as a dome, parquet floors, skylights, revolving storage space, and hiding beds.

When Thomas Jefferson, at age 33, wrote the Declaration of Independence with Benjamin Franklin, John Adams, and two others, he was one of the youngest delegates in the Continental Congress. The group spent about two weeks drafting the document. They presented it to the Congress on July 2, 1776. After making some changes, the Congress approved the document on July 4, 1776. The Declaration of Independence is greatly admired for its powerful cries for freedom and justice.

JAMES MADISON

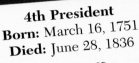

James Madison is known as the "Father of the Constitution," but he would disagree with the moniker. He claimed that the Constitution was not "the off-spring of a single brain," but "the work of many heads and many hands." Still, Madison is best remembered as one of the nation's Founders—those who helped create the United States of America.

Madison was born in Virginia to a wealthy, landowning family. He received an excellent education, studying government, history, and law. He quickly put his studies to use, often speaking out about the colonies seeking independence from England. Madison was a shy man, but he debated this issue with enthusiasm.

Madison served in the Virginia legislature before attending the Continental Congress, where he helped draft the outline for our system of government. He was also one of the writers of *The Federalist Papers*, which helped the new country's leaders accept the new Constitution. Madison became a representative in the first U.S. Congress. There he worked to pass the Bill of Rights, which outlines the basic rights of American citizens.

When Madison's close friend Thomas Jefferson was elected president, Madison became secretary of

4th President
Born: March 16, 1751
Died: June 28, 1836

Term of Office
1809 to 1817

Party
Democratic-Republican

Vice-presidents
1st term: George Clinton
2nd term: Elbridge Gerry

First Lady
Dolley Payne Todd Madison

Dolley Madison is remembered as one of the nation's favorite first ladies. She was a charming and intelligent woman who often gave fancy parties. People were quite surprised when the shy Madison married this lively woman.

Dolley Madison kept her cool during a crisis. As she was about to have a dinner party, she learned that British troops were on the way to the White House. Before fleeing, she packed up some White House treasures. The meal meant for Dolley's guests was later eaten by British troops—before they torched the president's house.

state. When Jefferson retired, he wanted Madison to follow him to the White House. Madison was elected. Soon the country faced war. The British were fighting France and took over U.S. cargo ships in the process. The War of 1812 was another war for independence, one the new nation was not prepared to fight. U.S. forces lost battle after battle on land and at sea. Finally, they saw victory at the Battle of New Orleans, leading many to think that the war had a successful end, though there was no clear victory on either side.

After serving two terms, Madison retired to his family home, Montpelier, and he spoke often about government issues. Madison died a few days before the nation began its sixtieth year.

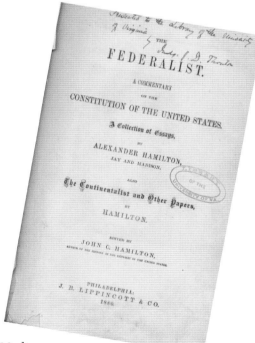

Madison had a hand in creating The Federalist Papers, *which were a group of 85 papers. They explained the importance of a strong central government for the nation. These papers convinced many leaders that the ideas presented in the Constitution were good ones.*

James Madison was not a man of great size. Standing at 5 feet 4 inches and weighing under 100 pounds, he was the shortest and lightest president. Madison was the first president to wear long pants. Before him, presidents wore knee pants.

The War of 1812 was fought on many fronts. America battled British forces at sea. On American soil, the British aided many Native American nations in their fight for territory against the U.S. government.

In 1814, the British took the nation's capital by force. They set fire to the Capitol, the president's home, and other buildings. The next morning, they intended to destroy the rest of the city, but a storm forced the British to retreat.

JAMES MONROE

James Monroe began his presidency with a trip across the country. At every stop, crowds cheered this former Revolutionary War officer. People said that Monroe brought the nation an "era of good feelings." It is how this president is best remembered.

Monroe, like three of the four presidents before him, was born in Virginia. When he was 16, his father died. For a time he went to college, but he left his studies to join the war for independence. After the war, Monroe studied law and opened a law practice. His energy and desire to achieve led him to a career in public service. He served in the Virginia Assembly, the Continental Congress, the U.S. Senate, and as governor of Virginia. He held national posts dealing with foreign relations under three presidents before him. In 1816, Monroe was elected president. In 1820, he was easily reelected. Monroe was known for his honesty. Thomas Jefferson said about him, "Monroe was so honest that if you turned his soul inside out there would not be a spot on it."

During Monroe's terms, the country faced great change. More states were being added to the nation. People began debating the

5th President
Born: April 28, 1758
Died: July 4, 1831

Term of Office
1817 to 1825

Party
Democratic-Republican

Vice-president
Daniel D. Tompkins

First Lady
Elizabeth Kortright Monroe

Monroe's 1817 inauguration was the first such ceremony held outdoors. Monroe began a tradition at his second swearing in. The U.S. Marine Band played at that inauguration, and it has played at every one since.

Monroe took a strong stand on foreign affairs. He followed Secretary of State John Quincy Adams's advice and issued a statement about other countries starting colonies in the Americas. Years later, this statement would bear Monroe's name—the Monroe Doctrine.

Elizabeth Monroe was thought to be one of the great beauties of her time. After they were married, the Monroes lived in France while James Monroe worked at a foreign relations post. The French called Mrs. Monroe la belle americaine, or "the beautiful American." Mrs. Monroe had a very formal manner, which made some people uncomfortable.

issue of slavery. Some people didn't want to admit any more states that allowed slavery into the union. Congress couldn't agree, but they finally reached the Missouri Compromise. It allowed Missouri to enter the union as a slave state while allowing Maine to enter as a free state. In affairs overseas, Monroe let other nations know that North America and South America were no longer open to Europeans wanting to start colonies.

At the end of his second term, Monroe retired to Virginia, the land he loved. He died some years later, on the Fourth of July—as had his friends Jefferson and Adams five years before.

When Monroe took the oath of office, the president's home was still being repaired. The British had nearly destroyed it with fire during the War of 1812. Monroe spent about four months traveling across the country. On this trip, he learned a great deal about the country and the people he would be governing.

In 1818, Congress voted that the U.S. flag should have 13 stripes to honor the original 13 colonies. During Monroe's term, five states would join the union: Mississippi, Illinois, Alabama, Maine, and Missouri.

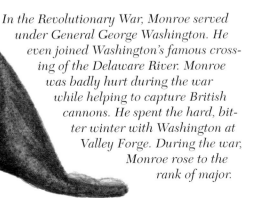

In the Revolutionary War, Monroe served under General George Washington. He even joined Washington's famous crossing of the Delaware River. Monroe was badly hurt during the war while helping to capture British cannons. He spent the hard, bitter winter with Washington at Valley Forge. During the war, Monroe rose to the rank of major.

19

JOHN QUINCY ADAMS

Early in life, John Quincy Adams developed a fierce love for and pride in America. He served his country from a young age until his death. Adams's career began with important posts overseas and ended with service in Congress. In between was a single term as president—the first ever for the son of a president.

Adams was born in Massachusetts. As a child, he watched the Battle of Bunker Hill in the Revolutionary War from a hill above his family farm. When his father, John Adams, was an important diplomat overseas, John Quincy Adams lived in Europe. Later, he graduated from Harvard and became a lawyer. Adams worked for each of the first five presidents, including his father. He was often America's spokesperson overseas. Although he did not have many friends, Adams was skilled at helping nations form good relationships. He helped make deals for the United States with other countries. Adams played an important role

6th President
Born: July 11, 1767
Died: February 23, 1848

Term of Office
1825 to 1829

Party
Democratic-Republican

Vice-president
John Caldwell Calhoun

First Lady
Louisa Catherine Johnson Adams

Louisa Adams was born and raised in England, making her the only first lady not born in the United States. Even in their family life, the Adamses were devoted to their country. They named one son George Washington Adams.

Adams didn't think it fitting to actively campaign for president by speaking for himself. There were quite a number of things Adams felt it was beneath him to do. He would not respond to attacks about him. But the things people said about him hurt him. He was very disappointed not to be reelected.

20

in writing the Monroe Doctrine. This was the statement the United States made to European countries to stay out of North and South America.

In 1824, Adams ran for president. None of the candidates earned the majority of votes, so the House of Representatives chose a winner— Adams. Many people were unhappy about this. They accused Adams of being dishonest. In fact, Adams was a man of great honesty. Adams ignored the attacks and tried to get things done as president. He wanted roads, canals, and schools built. But Congress would not do what Adams asked.

Adams did not win a second term as president, but later he ran for and was elected to the House of Representatives—the only president to do so after leaving the White House. For the next 17 years Adams served in Congress, representing Massachusetts, fighting for the things he believed in.

John Quincy Adams was the first president to have his photo taken. This early form of photography was invented in France by a man named Louis Daguerre. The photos were called daguerreotypes.

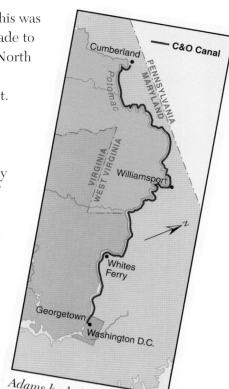

Adams had ideas about ways to help the new country grow. He urged Congress to build roads and canals to connect cities. While Congress didn't support most of his ideas at the time, he did manage to break ground on the C&O Canal in 1828. Most of the things Adams wanted would be done later. The C&O Canal was completed in 1850.

Adams's years in the White House were not happy ones for him. He was lonely. He passed the time by writing in his diaries, taking long walks, or swimming (often skinny-dipping) in the Potomac River.

ANDREW JACKSON

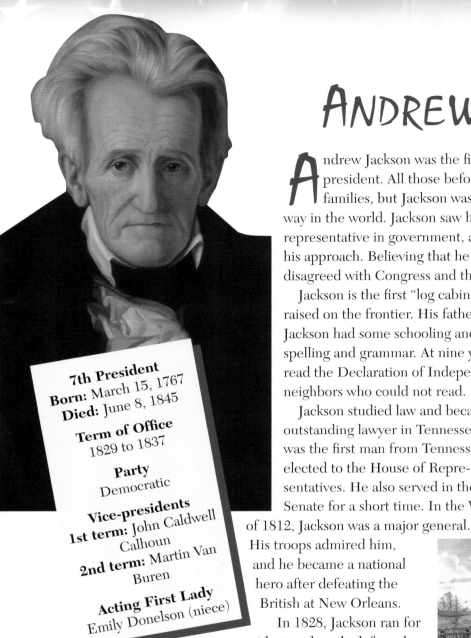

Andrew Jackson was the first common man to become president. All those before him had come from wealthy families, but Jackson was born poor and had to make his own way in the world. Jackson saw himself as the average American's representative in government, and the people loved him for his approach. Believing that he was the people's voice, he often disagreed with Congress and the Supreme Court.

Jackson is the first "log cabin" president, which means he was raised on the frontier. His father died just before he was born. Jackson had some schooling and learned to read, but he was weak at spelling and grammar. At nine years old, he read the Declaration of Independence to neighbors who could not read.

Jackson studied law and became an outstanding lawyer in Tennessee. He was the first man from Tennessee elected to the House of Representatives. He also served in the Senate for a short time. In the War of 1812, Jackson was a major general. His troops admired him, and he became a national hero after defeating the British at New Orleans.

In 1828, Jackson ran for president and easily defeated his rival, John Quincy Adams.

Jackson took bold action during his presidency, using his veto power regularly. He also made sure that presidents could choose their own cabinet members and replace them if they didn't follow orders. In 1832, Jackson was elected to a second term. At the end of this term, he was still as popular as when he first took office. Jackson retired to his home, the Hermitage, where he kept an eye on politics. Jackson died shortly after another man from Tennessee, James Polk, was elected president.

7th President
Born: March 15, 1767
Died: June 8, 1845

Term of Office
1829 to 1837

Party
Democratic

Vice-presidents
1st term: John Caldwell Calhoun
2nd term: Martin Van Buren

Acting First Lady
Emily Donelson (niece)

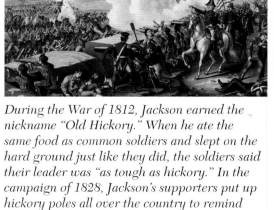

During the War of 1812, Jackson earned the nickname "Old Hickory." When he ate the same food as common soldiers and slept on the hard ground just like they did, the soldiers said their leader was "as tough as hickory." In the campaign of 1828, Jackson's supporters put up hickory poles all over the country to remind people of Old Hickory.

22

During Jackson's first inauguration, citizens flocked to the White House to see him. They trampled the furniture, cracked china, and some even had fistfights—making a mess of the White House. Jackson fled to the safety of a hotel while staff members served punch on the lawn to get the crowd out of the White House. Just before his term of office was over, Jackson threw a huge party where a wheel of cheese weighing 1,400 pounds was eaten by guests in about two hours. The White House smelled of cheese for weeks after Jackson moved out.

PETER COOPER'S LOCOMOTIVE, "TOM THUMB."

Railroads became important during Jackson's presidency. He was the first president to ride on a train. In 1830, the first passenger steam locomotive was built in the United States. The inventor, Peter Cooper, named the train Tom Thumb because it was just 20 feet long. After the Tom Thumb's first run on the track, some people suggested a horse race. It seemed as if the train would surely win, but the engine broke down and the horse pulled ahead.

At age thirteen, Jackson joined the Continental Army in the Revolutionary War, where he carried messages back and forth on horseback. Jackson is the last president to have fought in the Revolutionary War. He and his brother were captured, making Jackson the only president who was a prisoner of war. When Jackson refused to polish a British officer's boots, the officer attacked him, giving Jackson a scar on his face he carried the rest of his life.

Jackson's home, a mansion called the Hermitage, is near Nashville, Tennessee. Jackson was born in a simple log cabin in the wilderness. The difference in the two homes shows how successful Andrew Jackson was in his lifetime. Still, Jackson always felt that he was one of the regular people.

Some people didn't like Jackson's approach to being president. They said he was acting more like a king and called him King Andrew the First. Some people made fun of Jackson's lack of education. At one meeting, the speaker introduced him in Latin, which Jackson did not speak. Afterward, Jackson joked, "All the Latin I know is E pluribus unum." This motto appears on the U.S. seal and means "out of many, one."

23

Martin Van Buren

Martin Van Buren is the first president who was born a U.S. citizen. (The other presidents had been born before the new nation was formed.) Van Buren did much to change the way politics worked in the new nation. He went into the White House a popular man, but he lost popularity when the country had money problems.

Van Buren's parents were Dutch, and they settled in New York after coming to this country. Van Buren gained an early interest in politics. Political leaders often stopped by his parents' tavern. Van Buren loved their stories. He finished formal schooling early and was practicing law by age 21. Van Buren soon went into politics. After being elected to various state jobs, he built up a large group of supporters. He gave jobs to people who would vote for him. Van Buren served in the New York Senate, in the U. S. Senate, and as governor of New York. He supported Andrew Jackson for president and became his secretary of state when Jackson won the White House. When he was reelected, Jackson chose Van Buren as vice-president. Four years later, Van Buren ran on his own and won.

Soon after Van Buren took the oath of office, money became a problem. Banks closed. Businesses closed. People lost their jobs and could not find new ones. Van Buren did not cause the problems, but he did little to fix them. People voted him out of office.

Van Buren went back to his hometown in New York, but he did not give up on the presidency. He tried to win it back twice but was not successful.

8th President
Born: December 5, 1782
Died: July 24, 1862

Term of Office
1837 to 1841

Party
Democratic

Vice-president
Richard M. Johnson

Acting First Lady
Angelica Singleton Van Buren (daughter-in-law)

Martin Van Buren was born in Kinderhook, New York. He was sometimes called "Old Kinderhook." His supporters formed the O.K. Club. After a while, "OK" became a part of our vocabulary. It means "all right."

Van Buren continued something Jackson had started—forcing Native Americans to move from their homes to land the government set aside for them. As part of this plan, federal troops led about 15,000 members of the Cherokee nation from Georgia to what is now Oklahoma. This trip is called "The Trail of Tears" because many Cherokees died from the terrible conditions of the trip.

Early in Van Buren's term, the nation faced the money troubles known as the Panic of 1837. Many people lost everything they had worked for, including land and homes. People blamed Van Buren, but many of Andrew Jackson's policies led to the problem.

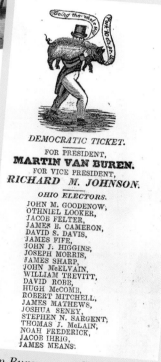

Van Buren was called the "Little Magician." This nickname came from his political success. He was always on the winning side of issues, and he made things happen for his supporters.

Martin Van Buren's wife, Hannah, died many years before he entered the White House. Van Buren wrote a book about his life, in which he failed to speak of Hannah at all. Van Buren did not marry again.

WILLIAM HENRY HARRISON

William Henry Harrison had something in common with George Washington and Andrew Jackson—he was elected president on his record as a war hero. But Harrison couldn't have been more unlike those two former presidents in terms of his time in office. Harrison had the shortest term in history: one month.

Harrison ran as a "log cabin" candidate, but he really came from a wealthy family. In fact, his father was one of the signers of the Declaration of Independence.

Harrison attended college and studied medicine. When his father died, he left medical school and became a soldier. He battled in the Indian Wars of the 1790s and earned honors for his bravery. Later, Harrison was appointed governor of the Indiana Territory. During that time,

9th President
Born: February 9, 1773
Died: April 4, 1841

Term of Office
March 1841 to April 1841

Party
Whig

Vice-president
John Tyler

First Lady
Anna Tuthill Symmes Harrison

Anna Harrison had not yet joined her husband in Washington when he died—she was still living in Ohio. Years later, Anna Harrison would become the only first lady to be the wife of one president and the grandmother of another— Benjamin Harrison.

Tecumseh was the chief of the Shawnee nation. He took a stand against settlers moving farther northwest and southwest. Harrison and Tecumseh met in battle at Tippecanoe during the Indian Wars of the 1790s and later at the Battle of the Thames, in Ontario, Canada, in the War of 1812. Tecumseh was killed in an 1813 battle.

The Whig party wanted to show that their candidate was different from Van Buren. Harrison was described as a hero who lived in a log cabin, while Van Buren lived in a palace—the White House. The image of Harrison wasn't true. He lived in a mansion, not a log cabin.

he led a battle against the Shawnee chief Tecumseh at Tippecanoe River. His victory brought him fame and earned him the nickname "Old Tippecanoe." Harrison fought again in the War of 1812 to defeat the combined British and Indian forces. He served in Congress, then left public life for his farm in Ohio. Then a new political party called the Whigs asked Harrison to run as president. In 1840, Harrison was elected.

Harrison delivered the longest inaugural address in history, running 1 hour and 40 minutes. Despite the chilly weather, Harrison refused to wear a coat or hat. Some people think this might have cost him his life. He caught a cold, which later turned into pneumonia. One month into his term, Harrison died. He was the first president to die while in office.

During the campaign of 1840, many people were unhappy with Van Buren because of the country's money problems. The Whigs promised that Harrison would improve things, but they didn't say how.

During Harrison's campaign, people remembered his war service. The catchy slogan "Tippecanoe and Tyler, Too!" referred to Harrison and his running mate, John Tyler, who later became president after Harrison's death.

THE REBOUND OF THE BALL.

JOHN TYLER

John Tyler was the first vice-president to take over for a president who had died. Although the Constitution was not clear about how a vice-president should take over for a president, Tyler set the standard. To help the transition of power, Tyler was sworn in, gave a brief inaugural address, and moved into the White House. Once in office, though, he was not as effective.

John Tyler was born in Virginia. He studied at William and Mary College and learned law. He held several offices, serving in the House of Representatives, as the governor of Virginia, and as a senator. When the Whigs wanted a Southern influence on their presidential ticket for the 1840 election, they turned to Tyler. He ran as Harrison's vice-president, and they won. Only one month later, Harrison died and Tyler became president.

10th President
Born: March 29, 1790
Died: January 18, 1862

Term of Office
1841 to 1845

Party
Whig

Vice-president
none

First Ladies
Letitia Christian Tyler
Julia Gardiner Tyler

In the mid-1840s, many people headed out west for Oregon. They packed up their belongings in covered wagons and hit the Oregon Trail. The trip took settlers over mountains, across deserts, and through Indian territory. Travel was slow and difficult. The 2,000-mile trek often took six months or more.

Tyler wanted increased power for states and less for the federal government, which made problems between the North and South worse. Tyler disagreed with Whig leaders on how banking should be handled, and he wouldn't back down on his beliefs. The Whigs then kicked Tyler out of their party.

Tyler encouraged people to settle in the West. He also made Texas, then an independent nation, part of the United States. He signed the resolution to admit Texas as a state on his last day in office.

With no party to back him, Tyler did not seek a second term. He retired to Virginia with his family. Firmly believing in the old Southern way of life, he helped create the Southern Confederacy during the Civil War. Tyler was elected to the Confederate Congress, but he died before serving.

Left: Julia Gardiner Tyler. Below: Letitia Christian Tyler.

Tyler's first wife, Letitia, died about a year after moving into the White House. Tyler later married Julia Gardiner, making him the first president to marry while in office. When Julia hosted a ball at the White House, Tyler joked about being an outcast of the Whig political party. "Now they cannot say that I am a President without a party," he said. From both marriages, Tyler had the most children of any president—15 in all.

Acting President Tyler
White House
Washington, D.C.

Tyler was called "His Accidency" because he took over for Harrison. Some people thought Tyler was an acting president, not a true president. Tyler insisted that he was a true president. He wouldn't even open mail that was marked "Acting President Tyler." After Tyler, people realized that vice-presidents should be ready to serve as president.

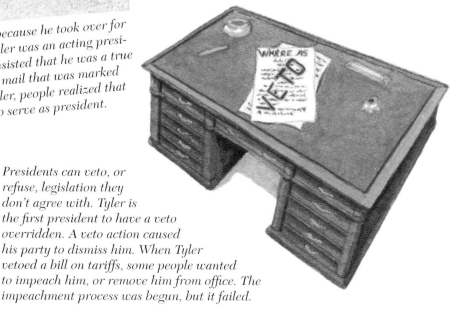

Presidents can veto, or refuse, legislation they don't agree with. Tyler is the first president to have a veto overridden. A veto action caused his party to dismiss him. When Tyler vetoed a bill on tariffs, some people wanted to impeach him, or remove him from office. The impeachment process was begun, but it failed.

JAMES KNOX POLK

James Polk focused his presidency on "manifest destiny," the popular belief that the United States should expand its borders from coast to coast. During his single term, Polk increased the size of the United States by two-thirds. Not since Thomas Jefferson's time had the country added so much to its land holdings.

James Knox Polk was born in North Carolina. After graduating from college with honors, he became a lawyer in Tennessee. Then Polk moved into politics, serving in the Tennessee legislature. Later, Polk was elected governor of Tennessee. When Polk was asked to run for president in 1844, it was a great surprise. People had expected another man to be chosen, but not everyone could agree on him. So Polk was chosen as a compromise candidate. He won the election and took office.

Polk focused his attention on the Oregon Territory, which was owned jointly by Britain and the United States. The United States set claim to the land, risking war. War was avoided, though, when the British agreed to give up most of that land. Then Polk looked to the

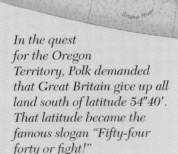

In the quest for the Oregon Territory, Polk demanded that Great Britain give up all land south of latitude 54"40'. That latitude became the famous slogan "Fifty-four forty or fight!"

11th President
Born: November 2, 1795
Died: June 15, 1849

Term of Office
1845 to 1849

Party
Democratic

Vice-president
George Mifflin Dallas

First Lady
Sarah Childress Polk

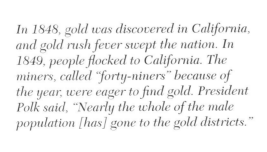

In 1848, gold was discovered in California, and gold rush fever swept the nation. In 1849, people flocked to California. The miners, called "forty-niners" because of the year, were eager to find gold. President Polk said, "Nearly the whole of the male population [has] gone to the gold districts."

Known as a charming hostess, First Lady Sarah Polk held the first official Thanksgiving dinner at the White House. Sarah Polk was also known for her intelligence. Her husband often consulted her on matters about the nation.

southern United States. Texas gained independence from Mexico in 1836 and became a state just before Polk became president. But the United States and Mexico couldn't agree on the state's borders. Polk also wanted to buy California, but Mexico refused to sell. Polk sent troops to Texas, and Mexico attacked. The U.S. Army battled successfully all the way from Texas to Mexico City. The war ended with the United States gaining the border it wanted in Texas, as well as getting New Mexico and California for $15 million. Polk was delighted to have the new territory, but it caused arguments in the country. Some thought slaves should be allowed in the new region, but others disagreed.

Polk left the White House after one term. He died three months later, in part because he had weakened his

In 1847, U.S. postage stamps replaced the practice of paying the postman. Also during Polk's administration, the U.S. Naval Academy was formed, and the Smithsonian Institution (pictured above) was created. Polk was the first president to have his inauguration reported by telegraph.

JAMES K. POLK.
THE PEOPLES CHOICE.

Polk was called a "dark horse," or unexpected candidate for president. His friendship with President Andrew Jackson helped him get chosen to run. Sometimes Polk was called "Young Hickory," since Jackson was known as "Old Hickory." Polk was so unfamiliar to most people that his opponent's campaign slogan, "Who is James K. Polk?," made a point about it.

GRAND NATIONAL DEMOCRATIC BANNER.

Polk set four goals for his presidency: lowering the tariff (taxes paid on goods brought into the country), setting up a national treasury, gaining the Oregon Territory, and making California part of the Union.

31

ZACHARY TAYLOR

War victories made Zachary Taylor a national hero and helped him win the presidency. A career soldier, Taylor had never before held an elected office. As an officer, he felt it was his duty to stay out of politics. However, a few years after leaving the battlefields, Taylor, who had never even voted in a presidential election, went to the White House. During Taylor's term, the nation disagreed strongly about the issue of slavery.

Taylor was raised on a plantation in Kentucky. He had little schooling on the frontier. Even as a child, he knew he wanted to be a soldier. He fought in the War of 1812, against the Seminoles in Florida, and in the Mexican War. During the Mexican War, Taylor led his troops to victory against amazing odds. He was greatly admired by his men.

The Whigs thought Taylor was a perfect candidate for president in 1848. After being elected, he was immediately

During Taylor's time, candidates did not attend political conventions. Instead, they waited at home for a letter. To inform Taylor of his nomination, the Whig party sent a letter. As was common at the time, the Whigs sent their letter with postage due, which meant that the person who received the letter would pay for postage. Taylor received many postage due letters from fans, and he had told the post office not to deliver them. So Taylor didn't receive the Whigs' letter. The Whigs figured this out and paid the postage to send Taylor another letter.

12th President
Born: November 24, 1784
Died: July 9, 1850

Term of Office
1849 to 1850

Party
Whig

Vice-president
Millard Fillmore

First Lady
Margaret Mackall
Smith Taylor

These bottles were given to voters when Taylor ran for president. But in fact he never truly wanted to be president. He agreed to run, but he still didn't want anyone to spend money on his campaign. He said he would only wish to be elected by the "spontaneous move of the people," not because of anything he did to win.

challenged by the question of slavery. People argued whether slavery should be allowed in the new western states won in the Mexican War. Taylor wasn't skilled at working with politicians. He was completely honest and was used to giving and taking orders. Taylor didn't know how to help people come to an agreement. He said what he thought, and Taylor thought that the new states should be allowed to decide for themselves. When Taylor's stand on slavery angered many people, he drew on his army experience. He said he would keep the country together by using troops if necessary.

No one knows what Taylor may have done. He died after completing a little more than a year in office.

Taylor's last words were, "I am about to die. I expect the summons very soon. I have tried to discharge my duties faithfully. I regret nothing, but I am sorry that I am about to leave my friends."

While many military leaders were concerned about handsome uniforms and polished boots, General Zachary Taylor often wore untidy farm clothes into battle. He was called "Old Rough and Ready" because of his appearance—and his willingness to fight side-by-side with his troops.

Zachary Taylor and his running mate, Millard Fillmore, seemed like complete opposites in their manner and dress. Taylor had short legs, paid little attention to dress, and had a relaxed style. Fillmore, on the other hand, was tall, handsome, and refined.

On Independence Day in 1850, President Taylor attended a celebration at the Washington Monument. Returning hot and tired, he is said to have enjoyed a snack of cherries and milk. Later he became ill. Many believe that the food was contaminated with bacteria. Taylor developed cholera and died five days later. Some people believe that Taylor was poisoned, but that has not been proved.

During Taylor's presidency, his horse, Old Whitey, could often be found grazing on the White House lawn. Tourists loved to see Taylor's old horse from the Mexican War. During Taylor's funeral, Old Whitey carried the president's boots backward in the stirrups and wore an empty saddle.

MILLARD FILLMORE

When Millard Fillmore became president upon Zachary Taylor's death, the debate about slavery was raging between the states. Fillmore's approach to the problem was different from Taylor's. Fillmore helped the states reach an agreement, which was called the Compromise of 1850. In the end, it only delayed the Civil War, and it cost Fillmore the support of his party.

Fillmore was born on a farm in the Finger Lakes region of New York. He worked on the farm until he was 15, when he went to work making cloth. Fillmore had a great desire to learn. He taught himself to read and attended school whenever he could. He studied law on his own and became a lawyer. He held state offices for many years and served in the U.S. House of Representatives.

In 1848, he ran as vice-president for Zachary Taylor. Just over a year later, Taylor died and Fillmore found himself in the White House working to help the states reach a compromise about slavery. That agreement is called the Compromise of 1850. With such a compromise, each side gets some of what it wants. This deal made California a free state, set borders for Texas, made New Mexico an official territory, allowed federal officers to help slave owners find runaway slaves, and stopped the buying and selling of slaves in the nation's capital.

As the Whig party began to fall apart, Fillmore retired to New York. He did not run for president until 1856, for a new party nicknamed the "Know-Nothing Party." He lost the election. Fillmore died many years later.

13th President
Born: January 7, 1800
Died: March 8, 1874

Term of Office
1850 to 1853

Party
Whig

Vice-president
none

First Lady
Abigail Powers Fillmore

Fillmore attended a one-room school. His teacher was almost his age, and he ended up marrying her. Abigail Powers had a huge effect on Fillmore's life. Educated on many topics, Abigail always encouraged and helped her husband. He often talked to her about important matters of state.

Fillmore was responsible for an important event known as "the opening of Japan." For years, Japan had refused to have any dealings with other countries. Fillmore sent Commodore Matthew Perry to visit the nation. Perry spoke with the Japanese ruler, who decided that trading ships from the United States could come into Japan.

BOSTON COURT HOUSE.

The Fugitive Slave Act was part of the Compromise of 1850, but it angered some Northerners so much that they vowed to work against Fillmore.

Reading was very important to First Lady Abigail Fillmore. She treasured books and was shocked to find no library when she moved into the White House. She convinced Congress to give her $250, then a large sum, to buy books for the mansion.

When Fillmore was 15 years old, he went to work for a cloth maker, as shown at right. He was an apprentice, or helper, who owed his employer a debt for learning the trade. Fillmore had to stay until the debt was paid. He borrowed $30 to pay for his freedom, and then he walked home—a distance of about 100 miles.

FRANKLIN PIERCE

When Franklin Pierce took over the presidency, things seemed to be going well between the states. The Missouri Compromise had helped quiet disagreements about slavery. It banned slaves in part of the country and allowed them in other parts. Pierce hoped to avoid more problems. His actions, though, only started more fighting and actually brought the country closer to civil war.

Pierce was born in New Hampshire to a well-known family. After college, he studied law. As a lawyer, Pierce became famous for his moving speeches. Then he went into politics. This was easy for Pierce because his father was already governor of his state. Pierce was elected to the New Hampshire legislature, and he won terms as a U.S. representative and senator. In Congress, Pierce became known as a man who paid more attention to his social life than his lawmaking.

When the Mexican War began, Pierce went to fight. Upon returning, he was asked to run for president. Pierce was the only man his party could agree on. He was handsome and charming, and he rarely

Pierce had already served in the House and Senate when the Mexican War broke out. Still, Pierce quickly enlisted to fight. He went in as a private, and he quickly rose through the ranks. During the war, Pierce was badly hurt when a horse threw him. Later Pierce faced his old war officer, Winfield Scott, in the battle for the presidency. Pierce won.

14th President
Born: November 23, 1804
Died: October 8, 1869

Term of Office
1853 to 1857

Party
Democratic

Vice-president
William Rufus De Vane King

First Lady
Jane Means Appleton Pierce

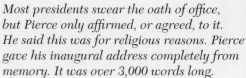

Most presidents swear the oath of office, but Pierce only affirmed, or agreed, to it. He said this was for religious reasons. Pierce gave his inaugural address completely from memory. It was over 3,000 words long.

Franklin Pierce was not the Democratic Party's first choice for president. In fact, it took 49 ballots for the party to pick a candidate at the 1852 convention. Pierce was a compromise. But he won the election and claimed the presidency.

Franklin Pierce's wife, Jane, did not enjoy public life. In fact, she fainted when she found out that he was running for president. The Pierce family faced great sadness just before Franklin Pierce took office. Their son was killed in a train accident. He was their third child to die. Mrs. Pierce could not cope and rarely left the White House. President Pierce was also extremely sad and had trouble concentrating on his duties.

took a stand on political matters. He made few enemies. In 1852, Pierce won the election.

As president, Pierce wanted to add more land to the United States. This brought up the question of whether the new areas would allow slaves. After much arguing, Pierce signed the Kansas-Nebraska Act. This brought an end to the Missouri Compromise. It allowed states to decide for themselves whether or not they would allow slavery. Bitter quarrels broke out, with people fighting to the death in Kansas.

Pierce was not asked to run again. He returned to New Hampshire, where he died 12 years later, almost forgotten.

NO GO AND GOING WITH A RUSH.

Winfield Scott was the Whig candidate for president in 1852. This cartoon shows how old "Fuss and Feathers," as he was called, fared during the campaign. Pierce is way out in front, and Scott is making no progress at all.

When Pierce signed the Kansas-Nebraska Act, fighting began. People in favor of slavery rushed to take charge of Kansas. People against slavery also wanted control of the state. Shooting started, earning the state the name "Bleeding Kansas." About 200 people died.

ECLIPSE & NO ECLIPSE   OR   TWO VIEWS OF ONE OBJECT.

JAMES BUCHANAN

I n his campaign for the presidency, James Buchanan was able to avoid the issue of slavery. He had been working for the government overseas, and he hadn't taken part in the public debates. But once in office, slavery became the focus of his presidency. He did not believe in slavery, but his actions favored those who did.

Buchanan's family had moved to this country from Ireland and did well as store owners. Buchanan graduated with honors from Dickinson College and then studied law. He was very successful as a lawyer, making a fortune before going into public service. Buchanan was elected to the state legislature, then the U.S. House and Senate. He also served as secretary of state and held important posts overseas. When Buchanan came back from England, he ran for president. He won a close election.

Two days after Buchanan took office, the Supreme Court made an important ruling about slavery. A slave named Dred Scott had argued that he should be free because his owner moved with him to a free state. The Court ruled against Scott; its decision supported slavery. The country became even more divided on the issue. Buchanan thought people should simply follow the laws. He also felt that the problem of slavery might fix itself. It only got worse.

15th President
Born: April 23, 1791
Died: June 1, 1868

Term of Office
1857 to 1861

Party
Democratic

Vice-president
John Cabell Breckinridge

Acting First Lady
Harriet Lane (niece)

Buchanan received the first international telegram when Queen Victoria of England sent him a message. Also, Buchanan was the first president to entertain a member of a royal family. Britain's Prince of Wales was a guest at the White House. Buchanan gave up his room for the prince and spent the night in a hallway.

Dred Scott was a slave in Missouri. His master's family moved to Illinois, where slavery was not allowed. Some lawyers wanted to help Scott gain his freedom, so they took his case to court. The Supreme Court decided that Scott had no right to sue because he was property, not a citizen. This ruling caused an uproar between the states.

SOUTH CAROLINA'S "ULTIMATUM".

JAMES BUCHANAN,
DEMOCRATIC CANDIDATE FOR PRESIDENT OF THE UNITED STATES.

James Buchanan had some problems with his sight. In fact, he had a different problem with each eye. One eye could see better up close. The other eye could see better far away. Buchanan would often tilt his head depending on which eye he needed to use.

Buchanan couldn't wait to get out of office. The final months of his presidency were the hardest. Buchanan wanted to keep the Union together, but he didn't feel the laws allowed him to force Southern states to stay.

At the end of Buchanan's term, Southern states began leaving the Union. Buchanan didn't feel he could stop them. In 1860, Buchanan did not run for reelection—his party did not nominate him. Abraham Lincoln took the White House. The only president who never married left the White House and went back to Pennsylvania.

Before becoming president, Buchanan had been in public service for about 40 years. Because he was an experienced politician, people expected great things. They thought he would find some way to end the arguments about slavery. At Buchanan's inauguration, guests ate about 1,200 gallons of ice cream before listening to his speech.

While Buchanan finished his term, Southern states (shown in gray) began breaking away from the United States. Seven states (shown in orange) seceded, or left the Union. They formed their own country, called the Confederate States of America. They elected Jefferson Davis as president in February 1861. A few months later, the Confederacy fired on Fort Sumter, and the War Between the States began.

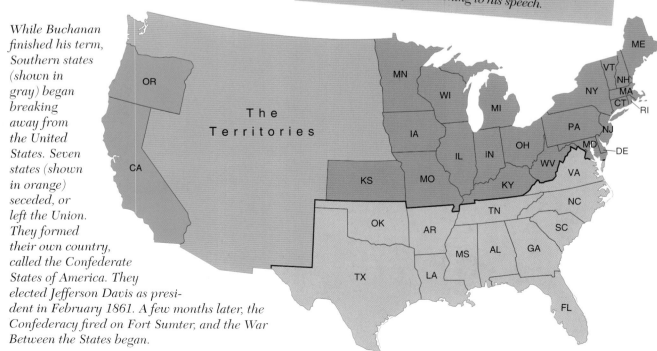

ABRAHAM LINCOLN

When Lincoln became president, the country was bitterly divided. The Northern states and the Southern states were arguing about slavery and states' rights. The two sides were threatening to go to war against each other—which they soon did. Lincoln is considered one of America's greatest presidents because he guided our nation through some of its darkest days and then brought the country back together again.

Lincoln was born in a log cabin in Kentucky. His frontier family barely scraped by. Lincoln hardly went to school, but unlike his father, he learned to read and write. Reading was a passion for Lincoln, and he taught himself many things by reading books.

As a young man, Lincoln worked on a flatboat, as a storekeeper, and as a surveyor before he was elected to the Illinois legislature. Then he taught himself law by studying law books. He was elected to Congress but lost two runs for the Senate. Later, his Senate campaign debates about slavery helped him become his party's candidate for president in 1860. Lincoln won the election

16th President
Born: February 12, 1809
Died: April 15, 1865

Term of Office
1861 to 1865

Party
Republican

Vice-presidents
1st term: Hannibal Hamlin
2nd term: Andrew Johnson

First Lady
Mary Todd Lincoln

Lincoln's family faced great personal loss in 1862 when their son Willie died in the White House of typhoid fever. Mary Lincoln was so grief-stricken that she could not cope. Later, when her husband was assassinated and another son, Tad, also died, her mental state became even worse.

1865

August: The North's General Sherman begins a campaign to take Atlanta.

September–November: The South abandons Atlanta, where its ammunition was stored.

November: The North's General Sherman begins the march across Georgia to the sea. President Lincoln is reelected.

January: The South falls.

February: The North's General Sherman marches through North and South Carolina, destroying everything along the way.

April: The South surrenders at Appomattox. President Lincoln is assassinated four days after the South's surrender.

During the election of 1864, Johnson ran as Lincoln's vice-president. Lincoln and Johnson carried the election. After Lincoln's death, Johnson continued the very difficult task of rebuilding and reuniting the country. Johnson didn't want to punish the South for seceding, but others did. Lawmakers disagreed so much with Johnson that they tried to impeach him and remove him from office. The Senate held an impeachment trial. By one vote, the Senate decided that Johnson had not committed a crime while in office.

When his term was up, Johnson was not asked to run again. He returned to Tennessee. Five years later, he was elected to the Senate. Several months after taking office, Johnson died.

Congress was so angry with Johnson that they passed laws to restrict what he could do. When Johnson fired his secretary of war, Edwin M. Stanton, he was said to have broken those laws. Congress brought charges to remove Johnson from office—the first impeachment trial in the nation's history. By a close vote, Johnson remained in office.

During Johnson's term, the United States bought Alaska from Russia for a sum of more than $7 million. At the time, many people thought this was foolish. When gold was discovered on Alaska's shores, people realized it had been a smart purchase.

When Johnson was president, he vetoed an important bill dealing with former slaves. It said they were citizens and outlawed unfair treatment of them. Congress overrode Johnson's veto. Also during Johnson's term, Congress began to discuss the Fourteenth Amendment to the Constitution, which stated that no state should "deprive any person of life, liberty, or property, without due process of law."

During the time known as "Reconstruction," or rebuilding after the Civil War, some dishonest people took advantage of the weakened system of government. Those who moved from the North to the South just to make money were known as "carpetbaggers." This name came from the suitcases made of carpet they took with them.

ULYSSES S. GRANT

After a war, a country often looks to its war heroes for leadership. In the first presidential election after the Civil War, the nation elected such a man—Ulysses S. Grant. Although a great military leader, Grant was not a great political leader.

Grant was born in Ohio, where his father owned a leather tanning shop. Although he didn't really want to, Grant attended the U.S. Military Academy at West Point. Later, he fought in the Mexican War. Grant eventually went back to work in his father's business and was there when the Civil War broke out. He commanded volunteer troops, gaining important battle victories for the North. In 1864, Lincoln promoted him to general in chief.

In 1868, Grant was a respected war hero and seemed a natural choice for president. Indeed, he won the election and reelection in 1872. During his terms, Grant faced the task of continuing Reconstruction, or the rebuilding and reuniting of the country. Congress passed the Fifteenth Amendment, which granted all men voting rights regardless of "race, color, or previous condition of servitude." Grant estab-

18th President
Born: April 27, 1822
Died: July 23, 1885

Term of Office
1869 to 1877

Party
Republican

Vice-presidents
1st term: Schuyler Colfax
2nd term: Henry Wilson

First Lady
Julia Boggs Dent Grant

During the Civil War, Grant earned the nickname "Unconditional Surrender," which matched his first and middle initials. Grant said "No terms except an unconditional and immediate surrender can be accepted," during the attack on Fort Donelson. Although thought of as a harsh leader, he was actually shy and sensitive.

Grant was known as a skilled horseman. He is the only president to have received a speeding ticket while driving a horse and carriage. Grant walked back to the White House after the officer impounded the carriage.

44

During Grant's world tour, he met other important leaders, including the queen of England and the emperor of Japan. Both Grant and the emperor had led troops as generals during civil wars.

Grant was an honest man, but scandal marked his first term as president. His vice-president, Schuyler Colfax, was dropped from the reelection ticket, and Henry Wilson joined Grant's ticket. During the campaign of 1872, Grant's supporters convinced people that Grant was a hardworking, upstanding man.

Passed during Grant's presidency, the Fifteenth Amendment guaranteed voting rights to former slaves. But still not all Americans could vote; women did not gain the right to vote until 1920.

lished the first national park, Yellowstone, in 1872. Grant skillfully helped the United States stay out of war with Great Britain. But Grant's terms were not without problems. There was a financial panic in 1873 that put many people out of work. Dishonest banking and tax deals were discovered. Although Grant was an honest man and was not directly involved in the deals, they still hurt his image.

After Grant left the White House, he toured the world. He tried his hand unsuccessfully at the banking business. A short time after the business failed, Grant died. He is buried in New York City, at the site commonly called Grant's Tomb.

Grant was deep in debt after his banking business failed. About this time, Grant found out that he had throat cancer. Grant didn't want to leave his family in debt, so he wrote a book about his life. He died just a few days after finishing the book. Mark Twain helped get the book published, and it earned Grant's family a great deal of money.

RUTHERFORD B. HAYES

Rutherford B. Hayes won the presidential election by just one vote, the closest election in U.S. history. Once in office, Hayes worked to make government honest and fair.

Hayes was born in Ohio. He did well in school, graduating from Kenyon College and Harvard Law School. He opened a law practice in Cincinnati and became a successful lawyer. When the Civil War called, Hayes fought bravely even though he had no military training. He was wounded in battle, and he had four horses shot out from under him. During the war, Hayes was nominated to run for Congress and accepted. He would not campaign, though. He said that anyone who left the battlefield to campaign "ought to be scalped." This statement probably helped him win the election. He went on to serve three terms as governor of Ohio.

In 1876, the Republicans chose Hayes to run for president, in part because of his war record. He was also known as a loyal and honest man. Still, most people

19th President
Born: October 4, 1822
Died: January 17, 1893

Term of Office
1877 to 1881

Party
Republican

Vice-president
William Almon Wheeler

First Lady
Lucy Ware Webb Hayes

The Hayes family hosted the first White House Easter egg roll. Children rolled painted Easter eggs along the White House lawn. The tradition continues today.

When President Hayes and his wife, Lucy Webb Hayes, moved into the White House, they ordered that wine and alcohol be removed. Mrs. Hayes earned the nickname "Lemonade Lucy" because she often served lemonade instead of liquor. Lucy Hayes was the first wife of a president to have graduated from college. She is also the first wife of a president to be called the "First Lady."

in the country expected the Democratic candidate, Samuel Tilden, to win. The popular vote and electoral vote were very close. There were reports of fraud, and it was unclear which candidate had the most votes. Congress spent months deciding, but finally the presidency went to Hayes in a deal known as the Compromise of 1877. Hayes kept up the terms of the deal by withdrawing federal troops from the South.

Hayes focused on changing some dishonest things in government. He chose honest men for his cabinet. He ordered that no government employees should be politicians. He tried to keep immigrants, those people moving to this country from another, safe.

Hayes had always said he would serve only one term. He returned to Ohio and died 12 years later.

The outcome of the election made things tense in the country. Because of this, Hayes took the oath of office in secret. The inauguration took place Saturday, March 3, 1877, in the Red Room of the White House. Hayes was the first president to take the oath at the White House. During his inaugural speech, Hayes said, "He serves his party best who serves his country best."

The inventor of the telephone, Alexander Graham Bell, installed the first phone in the White House while Hayes was president. The phone wasn't used much, since few other homes, offices, or businesses had phones. Hayes was also the first president to have a typewriter in the White House.

President Rutherford B. Hayes loved his home, Spiegel Grove, in Fremont, Ohio. For 20 years, he enjoyed making additions and improvements to the home. Spiegel Grove is now a presidential library. It is the country's first presidential library.

Rutherford B. Hayes wrote regularly in a diary from age 12 until his death at age 70. He was one of only three presidents known to record diary entries while in office.

JAMES A. GARFIELD

James A. Garfield served as president only a short time before he was killed. He was the second president to be shot while in office. During his six months in the White House, he worked to restore honor to the presidency and to the government.

Garfield was the last of the "log cabin presidents," those born on the frontier. Garfield's father died when the boy was two, but Garfield worked hard to earn money to go to school. After graduating from college in Massachusetts, Garfield went back home to Ohio to teach classical studies in college. In 1859, Garfield was elected to the Ohio Senate. A few years later, he led Northern troops in the Civil War and was recognized as a skilled military leader. He was promoted to major general. In 1862, Garfield was elected to Congress, but he didn't want to leave the military. President Lincoln convinced him to do so. Garfield then served in Congress for 18 years. He was known as a man of strong beliefs. "I would rather believe something and suffer for it, than to slide along into success without opinions," Garfield said.

20th President
Born: November 19, 1831
Died: September 19, 1881

Term of Office
March 4, 1881 to
September 19, 1881

Party
Republican

Vice-president
Chester A. Arthur

First Lady
Lucretia Rudolph Garfield

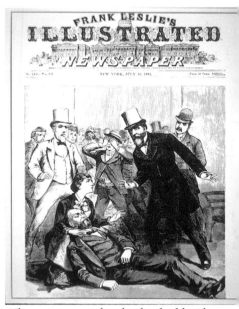

The nation was deeply shocked by the shooting of Garfield. As Garfield struggled to stay alive, people waited each day for reports of the president's progress. Garfield's killer was sentenced to hang.

As a young man, Garfield worked briefly on a canal boat. He fell overboard 14 times. Garfield survived all these mishaps even though he did not know how to swim. Garfield caught malaria and returned home. His mother nursed him back to health.

48

In 1880, Garfield ran for president and was elected. In office, he fought powerful leaders who wanted government jobs in return for political support. Instead, Garfield wanted government jobs awarded to people because of their abilities and experience. One person in particular was angry about Garfield's approach. He wanted a government job, but Garfield turned him down. At a Washington train station, the man shot Garfield. Several weeks later, the president died. As a result of Garfield's murder, people demanded better laws for how government jobs are assigned.

Garfield was a loving son. His mother lived with the family at the White House. Because she was frail, Garfield often carried his mother up and down the White House stairs. Garfield's wife was sick in bed for much of Garfield's presidency. She caught malaria from swamps behind the White House. She was in New Jersey recovering when she heard that her husband had been shot.

Garfield bought a run-down farmhouse and set about improving it for his family. He added many rooms and a porch, from which he gave many campaign speeches. An excellent speaker, he became known as the "Preacher President." Reporters named Garfield's home Lawnfield, because of its huge grounds. Reporters camped on the lawn during the campaign.

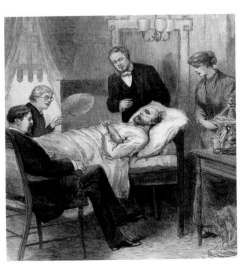

For weeks, doctors attended to Garfield in the White House. Later, he was taken by train to the New Jersey shore to escape the heat of summer in Washington. At times, Garfield seemed to improve, but the poor medical care of the day cost him his life.

Garfield was the country's first left-handed president. Actually, he could write with either hand. Some people say that Garfield could write Latin with one hand while writing Greek with the other.

CHESTER A. ARTHUR

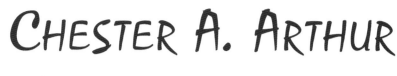

Chester A. Arthur's presidency was marked by surprise. First, people were shocked by James Garfield's death and Arthur's taking over as president. Then, people were surprised by what an effective leader Arthur became.

Arthur was born in Vermont, the son of a Baptist preacher. After graduating from college, Arthur became a teacher and later a lawyer. In 1871, President Grant appointed Arthur collector of the port of New York. His job was to collect fees for goods brought into the country. Arthur became known as a polite and friendly man. Along with his fancy tastes, his manner earned him the nickname the "Gentleman Boss." As the port collector, Arthur was associated with an important political leader, Roscoe Conkling. Conkling believed in rewarding political supporters with jobs and money.

Arthur had not held an elected office before he joined Garfield on the Republican ticket for vice-president in 1880. When he became president after Garfield's murder, Arthur decided it was time for change. He realized he could not support his old political

21st President
Born: October 5, 1829
Died: November 18, 1886

Term of Office
1881 to 1885

Party
Republican

Vice-president
none

Acting First Lady
Mary Arthur McElroy
(sister)

Immigration, or people moving to this country from another, was a big issue during Arthur's presidency. People were concerned that immigrants were taking away jobs from Americans. Arthur's administration passed the first federal law concerning immigration. It banned people from China from moving to the United States.

Upon Garfield's assassination, Arthur said, "All personal consideration and political views must be merged in the national sorrow. I am an American among millions grieving for their wounded chief." Arthur was sworn into office at his home in New York City.

Arthur didn't spend much time with his two children, but he loved to bring them out during the fancy parties he often gave. His love of the fine life led some to call him "Elegant Arthur." Arthur was known for changing clothes several times a day, for feasting with his friends, and for going fishing whenever he had the chance.

Arthur's wife, Nell, died before the 1880 election. To honor her memory, Arthur placed fresh flowers near her portrait in the White House each day. Arthur also donated a stained-glass window to a church where his wife had sung as a young girl. The president requested that the window be placed so he could see it at night from the White House.

friends. Instead, he worked to change the system of filling government jobs. He encouraged Congress to pass the Pendleton Act, which created a committee to oversee government workers.

At the end of his term, Arthur was battling a deadly kidney disease. He had learned of his condition after he had been president for about a year. When Arthur was not nominated for a second term, he retired to New York. He said, "Well, there doesn't seem to be anything else for an ex-president to do but go into the country and raise big pumpkins." He died less than two years after leaving the White House.

During his presidency, Arthur welcomed change, such as the Civil Service Commission. To get a government job, people would have to take a written test to show that they were the best-suited person for the position. New laws also prevented employees from being fired from a job because of who they supported politically.

Arthur was not pleased with the shabby condition of the White House. Arthur hired a famous New York designer, Louis Tiffany, to redecorate the White House.

Arthur is called the Father of the American Navy. In 1882, he pushed a bill through Congress to fund the construction of new all-steel ships.

GROVER CLEVELAND

Grover Cleveland is a president whose name is often linked with the word "only." He is the only president to be elected to two terms that were not back-to-back. He is the only president to be married in the White House. He is also the only president to have a baby born while living in the White House.

He was named Stephen Grover Cleveland at birth, but he later dropped his first name. Cleveland's father was a minister in New York. When Cleveland was 16, his father died, and Grover had to support his large family. In time, he became a lawyer. In a span of 11 years, Cleveland was elected sheriff, then mayor, then governor, and finally president. He won his first term by an extremely close vote. In the following election, he again won the popular vote. However, the presidency went to Benjamin Harrison because Harrison won the electoral vote. The next election brought Cleveland back to the White House after four years away.

Cleveland is known as a president who was honest and stood up for what he believed. He would not allow other officials to pass laws he didn't agree with. During his first term, Cleveland vetoed more than twice as many pieces of legislation as all previous presidents combined. During Cleveland's second term, the country hit hard economic times. Many people were out of work. Cleveland strongly believed that people should solve their own problems without help from the government.

After leaving the White House, Cleveland lived in New Jersey and taught at Princeton University. He died 11 years later, and his last words were, "I have tried so hard to do right."

22nd and 24th President
Born: March 18, 1837
Died: June 24, 1908

Terms of Office
1st term: 1885 to 1889
2nd term: 1893 to 1897

Party
Democratic

Vice-presidents
1st term: Thomas Andrews Hendricks
2nd term: Adlai Stevenson

First Ladies
Rose Elizabeth Cleveland (sister)
Frances Folsom Cleveland (wife)

Because of his size, Cleveland's nieces and nephews gave him the nickname "Uncle Jumbo." As governor of New York, Cleveland (seated on crate at right) earned another nickname by fighting corruption: "Grover the Good."

After her husband's defeat in 1888, it's said that Mrs. Cleveland told the White House staff that they would be back. Indeed they were. When Cleveland faced Benjamin Harrison again in a rematch, Cleveland won the election in both popular and electoral votes.

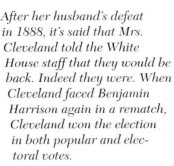

When the railroad strike interrupted mail delivery, Cleveland took action. He sent in federal troops to break up the strike. He said, "If it takes the entire army and navy to deliver one postcard in Chicago, that card will be delivered."

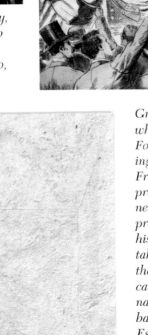

In 1886, Cleveland gave a speech dedicating the Statue of Liberty in New York City. The statue was a gift to America from the people of France.

Grover Cleveland was 49 years old when he wed 21-year-old Frances Folsom during his first term, making her the youngest first lady ever. Frances was the daughter of the president's old friend and law partner. Always dedicated to his job, the president did his duties as usual on his wedding day. The couple did take a five-day honeymoon. When the Clevelands' first child was born, candy makers borrowed her nickname "Baby Ruth" for their candy bar. The Clevelands' second daughter, Esther, was the only child of a president born in the White House.

BENJAMIN HARRISON

When the people went to the polls in 1888, they chose Grover Cleveland as their president. But Benjamin Harrison received more electoral votes, so he won the White House. As president, Harrison looked beyond our borders and worked to increase U.S. power in Latin America and the Pacific region. At home, he was challenged by problems with business, including the tariff, which is a tax on goods shipped into the country.

Harrison grew up in Ohio as part of a political family. When he was seven years old, his grandfather, William Henry Harrison, was serving in the White House. Harrison graduated from Miami University of Ohio and became an attorney in Indiana. During the Civil War, he served as a Union officer. He began his political career in the U.S. Senate. After one term, he was nominated for president. In the 1888 election, Harrison defeated Grover Cleveland with the electoral college victory.

In office, Harrison got Congress to approve a budget of $1 billion—at that point, it was the largest budget ever during times of peace. Harrison used the money to expand the navy,

23rd President
Born: August 20, 1833
Died: March 13, 1901

Term of Office
1889 to 1893

Party
Republican

Vice-president
Levi Parsons Morton

First Lady
Caroline Lavinia Scott Harrison

Benjamin Harrison was not a tall man, and his size prompted his soldiers in the Civil War to call him "Little Ben." When Harrison ran for president, his opponents tried to make it seem that he wouldn't be a good president. Harrison's camp argued that "Grandfather's Hat Fits Ben," meaning that he could be president, just as his grandfather had been.

Harrison was the first president to use electricity in the White House. At the time, many people did not understand how electricity worked. It's said that Harrison was afraid to touch the switches, so many lights stayed on through the night.

build steamships, and improve harbors. President Harrison signed the Sherman Anti-Trust Act to prevent a single group of owners from controlling a whole industry.

Harrison tried to protect American businesses with a high tariff. Harrison advanced American interests overseas, too. He arranged for a number of trade agreements in which nations promised to trade with the United States if our country traded with them. He also agreed to protect the island of Samoa. Harrison worked to gain control of land in Panama so the United States could build a canal, or waterway, to link the Atlantic and Pacific oceans.

In 1892, Harrison lost his bid for reelection to Grover Cleveland. He retired to Indianapolis, where he returned to the practice of law. He remained active in public life until his death.

Harrison loved animals of all sorts and had plenty of pets, including dogs, horses, and an opossum, for his grandchildren. He also had a goat, named Old Whiskers, who pulled the children in a cart around the White House lawn.

Benjamin Harrison was not a very outgoing man. In fact, some called him "the human iceberg." He was a deep thinker and didn't enjoy crowds. When running for president, he stayed home and gave speeches to small groups from his own front porch. He was popular among those who had fought in the Civil War because of his own record of service.

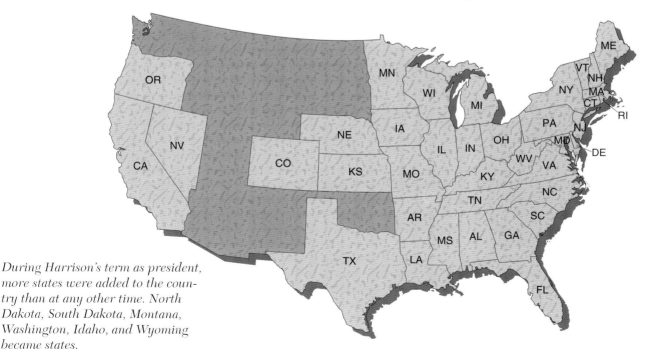

During Harrison's term as president, more states were added to the country than at any other time. North Dakota, South Dakota, Montana, Washington, Idaho, and Wyoming became states.

WILLIAM McKINLEY

William McKinley was the last president who served in the Civil War. Another war, the Spanish-American War, would be an important part of McKinley's term in office. McKinley helped the United States become a world power.

McKinley, like several presidents before him, was born and raised in Ohio. He planned to become a minister, but the Civil War called him to duty. He was a brave soldier, earning the rank of brevet major under Colonel Rutherford B. Hayes. After the war, McKinley became a lawyer. He entered politics, serving in Congress and becoming governor of Ohio. In 1896, McKinley ran for president. Known as an excellent speaker, McKinley campaigned from his own front porch. His wife had health problems, and he would not leave her to travel the country.

In office, McKinley turned his attentions to U.S. relationships with other countries. Cuba was trying to get out from under Spain's rule. Some people thought the United States should stay out of those problems. But when the U.S. battleship *Maine* was attacked in Cuba, Congress declared war. The Spanish-American War ended four months later with a U.S. victory. After the war, the United States took control of

25th President
Born: January 29, 1843
Died: September 14, 1901

Term of Office
1897 to 1901

Party
Republican

Vice-presidents
1st term: Garret Augustus Hobart
2nd term: Theodore Roosevelt

First Lady
Ida Saxton McKinley

The man who shot McKinley was an out-of-work laborer. He claimed to be an anarchist, or someone who is against government. The man was found guilty of murder.

McKinley (far left), shown here with his cabinet, focused on U.S. relations with foreign countries. To set up trade with China, McKinley had Secretary of State John Hay (center in photo) send notes to European countries and to Japan saying the United States supported China's independence. They encouraged equal status for all nations that wanted to trade with China. This was called the Open Door Policy.

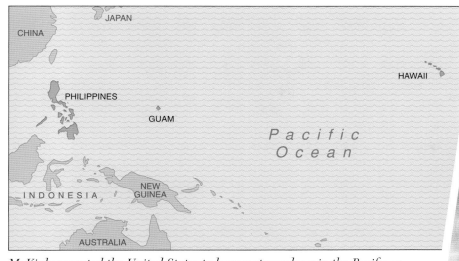

McKinley wanted the United States to have a strong base in the Pacific so our country could trade with China. Guam and the Philippines were the start of the base. McKinley expanded the base by annexing, or taking over, the Hawaiian Islands.

McKinley's first vice-president died during their first term. Theodore Roosevelt joined McKinley's ticket in 1900. Roosevelt campaigned with enthusiasm. "Four Years More of the Full Dinner Pail" was the slogan to remind people that the country was doing well.

Puerto Rico, Guam, and the Philippine Islands. Later, McKinley sent troops to China to help stop a rebellion.

The nation did well under McKinley, and he was reelected. Six months into his second term, McKinley attended the Pan-American Exposition, a huge fair, in Buffalo, New York. McKinley was shaking hands with people in the crowd when a gunman fired two shots at him. McKinley died eight days later.

McKinley was devoted to his wife, Ida. When McKinley was shot, his first words were for his wife. "My wife, . . . be careful how you tell her—oh be careful."

McKinley was familiar with war, and he didn't want to encourage another one. In his first inaugural address, he said, "War should never be entered upon until every agency of peace has failed." Before the United States declared war with Spain, newspapers were printing terrible reports about how Spain was mistreating Cubans. Not everything printed was true, but the stories led people to want war to stop the cruelty. When the U.S. battleship Maine *was attacked, Americans were outraged. "Remember the* Maine!*" became a familiar cry.*

57

THEODORE ROOSEVELT

Theodore Roosevelt became the youngest president ever when he took over after William McKinley's assassination. Bursting with energy and enthusiasm, Roosevelt brought his unique way of seeing and doing things to the presidency. He is the first vice-president to succeed a president and later be elected in his own right.

Roosevelt was the son of a wealthy New York family. Right after graduating from Harvard, he married and was elected to the state legislature. A few years later, Roosevelt faced tragedy when his wife and mother died on the same day. To work through his grief, he moved to the Dakota Territory and became a cowboy. In the West, he earned a tough reputation.

Two years later, Roosevelt moved back to the East Coast. He married again and went back into public service. At this time, Cuba was fighting Spain for independence. When America joined the war in 1898, Roosevelt put together a group of volunteers called the Rough Riders. They became famous for their fearless charge up San Juan Hill. Press reports of this attack helped Roosevelt get elected governor of New York. In 1901, Roosevelt served as vice-president and then president. Roosevelt worked to make sure every American received a "square deal"—fair wages for their work, fair prices for

26th President
Born: October 27, 1858
Died: January 6, 1919

Term of Office
1901 to 1909

Party
Republican

Vice-president
1st term: none
2nd term: Charles Warren Fairbanks

First Lady
Edith Kermit Carow Roosevelt

In 1902, Theodore Roosevelt, nicknamed Teddy, went on a bear hunt in Mississippi. The only bear he found was just a cub, and he refused to shoot it. A newspaper ran a cartoon about this. Then a toy maker in Brooklyn put the cartoon next to a stuffed bear, calling it "Teddy's Bear." The teddy bear was born.

DRAWING THE LINE IN MISSISSIPPI

A sickly child who suffered from asthma, Roosevelt was tutored at home until he entered Harvard. By that time, he had improved his health by exercising endlessly. He loved all forms of exercise, especially swimming, horseback riding, hiking, and boxing. While he was president, he often boxed with professional sparring partners to keep in shape.

Roosevelt's love of the outdoors led him to preserve the environment. Roosevelt established hundreds of acres of national parks and forests, many of them in the Northwest and Alaska.

The Roosevelts were known as a rowdy, fun-loving family, even in the White House. Quentin Roosevelt once took his pony, Algonquin, on the White House elevator to visit his brother Archie, who was sick in bed. The young Roosevelts also roller-skated in the White House and slid down the banisters on serving trays. They kept a variety of pets, including snakes, parrots, bear cubs, and a lion cub.

goods and services, and protection from impure foods and drugs.

Roosevelt won the 1904 election in a landslide. When that term was up, he wanted to stay in office but had said that he would not run in 1908. He did run, though, in 1912 for a new party he called the Progressive Party. But Roosevelt was defeated and went into retirement, writing an autobiography and exploring jungles in Brazil. Roosevelt died a few years later.

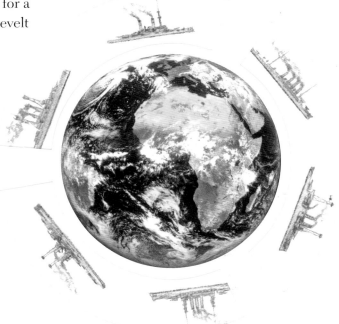

People had long wanted a waterway to connect the Atlantic and Pacific oceans across Central America. Ships could then avoid the long, difficult sail around Cape Horn on South America's southern tip. Theodore Roosevelt was successful in buying the canal zone from the newly independent nation of Panama. Roosevelt's trip to Panama to observe the construction was the first overseas trip by a president in office.

Roosevelt was once the assistant secretary to the navy, and he believed in building a strong naval force. In dealing with other countries, Roosevelt thought the United States should "speak softly and carry a big stick." For Roosevelt, the navy was part of the "big stick." He convinced Congress to build new ships to create a powerful navy. To show the world this mighty force, Roosevelt sent the navy on a cruise around the world.

WILLIAM HOWARD TAFT

William Howard Taft followed a very popular president: Theodore Roosevelt. Although Roosevelt had a hand in Taft getting elected, he proved a hard act to follow. Taft never really wanted to be president in the first place—the work he loved was the law.

Taft grew up in Ohio, the son of an important judge. Taft graduated from Yale and practiced law, taught law, and served as a judge. In 1900, President McKinley chose Taft to be an administrator for a new territory in the Pacific, the Philippine Islands. Taft worked to get roads, schools, and better conditions in the area.

Then Roosevelt asked Taft to serve as secretary of war. In this post, Taft managed the construction of the Panama Canal.

Roosevelt and Taft became good friends. Roosevelt decided that Taft should follow him as president in 1908. Taft didn't really want to run, but his wife also encouraged him. People thought Taft would continue Roosevelt's plans, so they voted for him, and he won. Taft continued making sure big business was fair and that people had good conditions in which to live and work. But Taft did things his own way, not

President Taft put the White House "on wheels" by changing its stables into a garage for four cars.

27th President
Born: September 15, 1857
Died: March 8, 1930

Term of Office
1909 to 1913

Party
Republican

Vice-president
James Schoolcraft Sherman

First Lady
Helen Herron Taft

As a child, Taft was often called Big Lub. Later, he was known as Big Bill. Taft was the heaviest president, weighing well over 300 pounds. Taft once got stuck in the White House bathtub. After that, he had a special oversized tub installed— one big enough to hold four men.

with Roosevelt's flashy style. Some people thought Taft wasn't being true to Roosevelt's ideas, and Taft became unpopular. Even Roosevelt was not pleased and decided to run again against Taft in the election of 1912. Both Roosevelt and Taft were defeated in that race. Taft was glad to leave the White House. He taught law at Yale until he was appointed chief justice of the United States Supreme Court in 1921. He served in this position until just before he died.

Taft is the only man in U.S. history to serve as both president and a Supreme Court justice. He considered the Supreme Court appointment the highest honor and enjoyed that position much more than being president. Taft wrote, "I don't remember that I ever was president."

It is said that Helen Taft encouraged her husband to run for president because she wanted to be first lady. She was the first wife of a president to take part in the inaugural parade. She later wrote a book about her years in the White House—it was the first book of its kind. The Tafts were the first presidential couple (and are still one of only two couples) to be buried in Arlington National Cemetery.

Taft loved to play golf. That may have been part of the reason he became unpopular. Some people felt the president shouldn't spend time on a rich man's sport. Although it was not noticed at the time, Taft did a great deal for the country. He made sure federal lands containing oil and coal were protected. He got laws passed that set up a federal income tax and that allowed senators to be elected directly by citizens.

As a child, Taft loved to play baseball. He was a great hitter but not a great runner because of his size. Later, Taft began the tradition of the president throwing out the first ball on baseball's opening day.

61

WOODROW WILSON

Woodrow Wilson was a forward-thinking man. As president, he got Congress to pass many important laws. He helped the United States avoid conflict in World War I as long as possible. After entering the war, Wilson rallied Americans and their resources to help gain victory. He designed a plan for lasting world peace called the League of Nations. Woodrow Wilson is remembered as one of the country's great presidents.

28th President
Born: December 29, 1856
Died: February 3, 1924

Term of Office
1913 to 1921

Party
Democratic

Vice-president
Thomas Riley Marshall

First Ladies
Ellen Louise Axson Wilson (first wife)
Edith Bolling Galt Wilson (second wife)

Wilson grew up familiar with war. He was born in Virginia and was raised in Georgia. As a child, Wilson saw Yankee soldiers marching through his town during the Civil War.

Wilson graduated from Princeton. He also studied law and later earned an advanced degree from Johns Hopkins. He became a professor at Princeton and then its president. Wilson was known as a man who wanted change and would not shy away from problems.

Wilson was able to get some important laws passed, including the Underwood Act, which lowered tariffs on imported goods. The Federal Reserve Act set up a board to control the money supply. The Federal Trade Commission prevented unfair business practices. Other laws blocked businesses from making children work and regulated how many hours workers could be on the job.

Armistice Day
November 11

On the day before Wilson's first inauguration, suffragists, or women who were fighting for the right to vote, held a parade. They wanted to bring attention to their cause. Over 5,000 women marched down Pennsylvania Avenue. The parade ended in a near riot.

62

President Wilson (right) takes a short break from the Peace Conference with (from left to right) D. Lloyd George of Great Britain, Vittorio Orlando of Italy, and Georges Clemenceau of France.

At the end of World War I, Wilson traveled to Paris to help make peace. He was the first president to go to Europe while in office. Wilson presented the Treaty of Versailles to other world leaders, who agreed to the terms for peace. Wilson later presented the Treaty to the Senate and challenged them, "Dare we reject it and break the heart of the world?" The Senate did not accept the Treaty, so the United States did not become part of the governing body for world peace. Still, Wilson won a Nobel Peace Prize for his efforts.

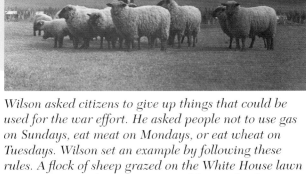

In 1910, he became governor of New Jersey. By 1912, Wilson was in a race for president against Taft and Theodore Roosevelt. Wilson won.

When World War I erupted in Europe, the United States didn't take sides. Wilson won a second term. Shortly after that, Germans sank a U.S. ship, the *Lusitania*. Wilson felt that the country could no longer stay out of the war. "The world must be made safe for democracy," he said. American efforts helped the Allies win the war.

Wilson worked hard for world peace, writing a treaty to set up the terms for peace. The treaty was not approved by Congress. Wilson was under great stress, and he suffered a stroke. Although Wilson was very ill, his second wife helped him continue as president (his first wife died during his first term). Wilson's health remained poor, and he died a few years after leaving the White House.

Wilson asked citizens to give up things that could be used for the war effort. He asked people not to use gas on Sundays, eat meat on Mondays, or eat wheat on Tuesdays. Wilson set an example by following these rules. A flock of sheep grazed on the White House lawn to save the gas a lawn mower would use. The sheep's wool was sold to raise money for the Red Cross.

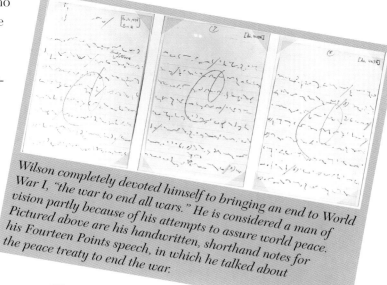

Wilson completely devoted himself to bringing an end to World War I, "the war to end all wars." He is considered a man of vision partly because of his attempts to assure world peace. Pictured above are his handwritten, shorthand notes for his Fourteen Points speech, in which he talked about the peace treaty to end the war.

63

WARREN G. HARDING

Friends often said that Warren G. Harding looked like a president. When Harding took office, he found that looking like a president was much easier than actually being one. Harding was a likable man with many friends. His friends did him no favors, though, when he was in the White House. Instead, many of them brought about scandals. The scandals were just being discovered when Harding died suddenly in the middle of his term.

Harding grew up in Ohio and went to college there. Soon after graduating from college, Harding became a newspaper owner. This led to him serving in the Ohio state legislature, as Ohio's lieutenant governor and governor, and in the U.S. Senate. Throughout his career, Harding was well liked. He didn't take a stand on any issues, so he upset no one. In 1920, he ran for president with the slogan "A Return to Normalcy," after World War I. Harding won by a landslide.

29th President
Born: November 2, 1865
Died: August 2, 1923

Term of Office
1921 to 1923

Party
Republican

Vice-president
Calvin Coolidge

First Lady
Florence Kling De Wolfe Harding

Both of Harding's parents were doctors. He had one sister who grew up to be a police officer in Washington, D.C. At age 24, Harding suffered a nervous breakdown and had to spend time in a mental hospital.

Harding was the first president to speak on the radio. The broadcast honored Francis Scott Key, who wrote "The Star-Spangled Banner."

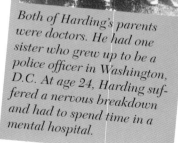

Harding had a loyal dog named Laddie Boy. Each morning, Laddie Boy brought Harding the newspaper. After President Harding died, newspaper workers across the nation collected pennies to pay for a statue of Laddie Boy. The statue can be seen at the Smithsonian Institution.

Harding loved partying and keeping late nights with his friends. Playing poker was a favorite activity of his. President Harding once gambled the White House china in a poker game—and lost it!

Harding's presidential election was the first in which women could vote. Harding was also the first president to ride to his inauguration in an automobile. Harding used a new invention, the megaphone, to give his inaugural address to the nation. A megaphone makes sounds louder.

In the White House, Harding knew that this important job was too much for him. He understood little about running the country, and he left much of it to others. Harding appointed many friends to his cabinet. Some were honest men, but many were not. They set out to get rich at the expense of the government. When Harding understood what was happening, he was deeply troubled. He set out on a trip across the country to explain to the American people that he was an honest man. During the trip, Harding suddenly became ill and died. Some people claimed that his wife had poisoned him to spare him embarrassment. These claims were not proven, though. Most people believe Harding died of natural causes.

Things went well for Harding as a newspaper owner. At age 25, he married Florence Kling De Wolfe, who ran the newspaper with him. Her work helped the newspaper make money, which allowed Harding to run for office.

Just after Harding's death, the Teapot Dome scandal was uncovered. One of Harding's cabinet members allowed private companies to drill for oil on public lands in Wyoming's Teapot Dome reserve. In exchange for granting these rights, the man was given huge sums of money. Harding did not know about this arrangement. Later, the cabinet member was sent to jail.

CALVIN COOLIDGE

Calvin Coolidge was visiting family in Vermont when he learned that Warren Harding had died suddenly, making Coolidge president. So Coolidge placed his hand on a family Bible and was sworn in by his father, who was a notary public. In leading the nation, Coolidge held to the high standards of behavior of his New England childhood. Coolidge helped restore American's faith after the scandals of the Harding presidency.

Coolidge, the son of a storekeeper, grew up in Vermont. He graduated from Amherst College with honors. He practiced law and entered politics in Massachusetts. He began with local offices and rose from councilman to governor of Massachusetts. In 1920, he was elected vice-president with Harding as president. After Harding's death in 1923, Coolidge moved into the White House.

During Coolidge's presidency, the Harding scandals were uncovered. Harding had people working for him who were more interested in what they could gain than in what they could do for the country. Coolidge quickly replaced dishonest staff members with honest ones.

Under Coolidge, the country did very well in money matters. Stocks, prices, and wages all went up. Coolidge was known as a man of few words and simple ideals. He said that "When things are going all right, it is a good plan to let them alone." Coolidge won reelection in 1924. Things continued to go well, but when it was time for reelection, Coolidge said, "I do not choose to run for President in 1928." Instead, he retired to Massachusetts. He was surprised by the financial problems that soon followed. Just before his death, he said, ". . . I no longer fit in with these times."

30th President
Born: July 4, 1872
Died: January 5, 1933

Term of Office
1923 to 1929

Party
Republican

Vice-president
1st term: none
2nd term: Charles Gates Dawes

First Lady
Grace Anna Goodhue Coolidge

President Coolidge was known as a man of few words and was nicknamed "Silent Cal." The White House staff, on the other hand, nicknamed First Lady Grace Coolidge "Sunshine" because of her bright outlook on life.

Coolidge was on vacation at his family's home when Harding died in San Francisco. The Coolidge family had no telephone, so a messenger was sent to inform the vice-president. Coolidge learned the news after midnight. He took the oath of office at his home just before 3:00 A.M.

In retirement, Coolidge wrote the story of his life. Not surprisingly, for Coolidge was a man of few words, the book was quite short.

The Autobiography
OF
CALVIN COOLIDGE

New York
COSMOPOLITAN BOOK CORPORATION
1929

Although he didn't say much, Coolidge seemed to enjoy meeting guests at the White House. He was often photographed greeting people while in costume. Despite being quiet, Coolidge could be quite funny. At a White House dinner party, one guest told Coolidge of a bet she made. She explained that she bet she could get the president to say more than two words. "You lose," Coolidge said.

Coolidge did much to promote the flight industry. In 1926, he helped get the Air Commerce Act passed. The act allowed the government to help the new industry.

Coolidge gained the national spotlight as governor of Massachusetts. When Boston police went on strike and crime raged out of control, Coolidge fired the officers and sent in state troopers. When Samuel Gompers (pictured at left), president of the American Federation of Labor (AFL), asked him to reconsider, Coolidge sent Gompers a telegram that said, "There is no right to strike against the public safety by anybody, anywhere, anytime." The telegram earned Coolidge the reputation as a no-nonsense leader.

HERBERT HOOVER

When Herbert Hoover was running for president, he promised "a chicken for every pot and a car in every garage." He wasn't able to deliver. During Hoover's term, the stock market crashed and America plunged into the Great Depression. People were angry about the tough economic times, and they blamed Hoover, perhaps unfairly.

Hoover was born in Iowa. Both his parents died by the time he was nine, and he lived with relatives in Oregon. He graduated from Stanford University with a degree in geology (the study of the earth). Hoover became a mining engineer and traveled around the world in search of minerals. When he was in London, he helped get Americans out of Europe at the start of World War I. President Wilson named Hoover head of the Food Administration. It was Hoover's job to get people to cut down on how much food they used so there would be enough to send to troops overseas. Hoover managed things well. Later, Hoover served as secretary of commerce to presidents Harding and Coolidge.

In 1928, Hoover ran for president. People learned that he had worked hard and had made himself a fortune. He inspired hope, encouraging Americans to create a "new day" for the country. Hoover

31st President
Born: August 10, 1874
Died: October 20, 1964

Term of Office
1929 to 1933

Party
Republican

Vice-president
Charles Curtis

First Lady
Lou Henry Hoover

People blamed Hoover for the Great Depression. They used his name to describe many things linked to the bad times. People called groups of shacks where people lived "Hoovervilles." They called newspapers that people used to keep themselves warm "Hoover blankets." They called wild jackrabbits that they caught for food "Hoover hogs."

won the election. Within months, the stock market crashed. Banks closed, and people lost whatever money they had in them. Many jobs were wiped out, and people had no way to earn money. Many people couldn't pay for a place to live or food to eat. Hoover did not seem to understand how bad things were. He believed the downturn was part of the business cycle and that it would take care of itself.

Hoover did not win reelection. He did, however, help out presidents Truman and Eisenhower when they asked him. Hoover enjoyed the longest retirement of any president—31 years.

October 24, 1929, the day the stock market crashed, became known as "Black Tuesday." Although Hoover didn't understand how desperate Americans were, he tried to cut presidential expenses. He did not receive any pay for his work as president. He turned the presidential yacht over to the Navy. He shut down the White House stables.

During World War I, Hoover ran a campaign to get Americans to save food and other goods so that the supplies could be sent to troops fighting in Europe. His name was made into an action word—to "hooverize" meant to use as little of something as possible.

Herbert Hoover married the only female geology student then attending Stanford. They traveled all over the world together and learned many languages. In the White House, they sometimes spoke Mandarin Chinese when they did not want others to know what they were saying.

Hoover directed many relief efforts overseas. When he and his wife were in China, they were caught in a revolt. Hoover put himself in great danger when he rescued some Chinese children. He helped feed people in Europe before and after World War I.

FRANKLIN D. ROOSEVELT

During the longest presidency in history, Franklin Roosevelt expertly steered the country through national and world crises. He is known as one of the country's greatest presidents.

Franklin Roosevelt was born into a wealthy family from New York. He went to the best private schools and universities. By the time he began practicing law, he had married Eleanor Roosevelt, a distant cousin.

Roosevelt wanted to serve his country through politics. In 1910, he was elected to the New York Senate. Later he became assistant secretary of the U.S. Navy. In 1920, Roosevelt ran for vice-president, but his party was defeated. Then, in 1921, Roosevelt contracted polio, a disease that paralyzed his legs. He showed great courage as he fought for recovery. Roosevelt returned to politics seven years later and became governor of New York.

32nd President
Born: January 30, 1882
Died: April 12, 1945

Term of Office
1933 to 1945

Party
Democratic

Vice-presidents
1st and 2nd terms:
John Nance Garner
3rd term: Henry Agard
Wallace
4th term: Harry S.
Truman

First Lady
Anna Eleanor Roosevelt

President Roosevelt's dog, Fala, went everywhere with him. The Secret Service nicknamed the dog "the Informer" because they knew that when they saw Fala, the president was sure to be nearby.

Franklin Roosevelt's family was quite well-known. In fact, he had a relative who had already served as president—Theodore Roosevelt. Franklin greatly admired his distant cousin Teddy. As a youngster, Franklin was a pampered only child. As did many boys of the time, he wore only dresses and kilts until he was eight years old. He often traveled to Europe with his parents.

During World War II, Roosevelt met with Winston Churchill of Great Britain (seated to left of Roosevelt) and Joseph Stalin of Russia (seated to right) to discuss the war. These leaders were known as "The Big Three." Although this was a serious time, Roosevelt's friendly nature came through. He joked with the men, even calling Stalin "Uncle Joe."

At her wedding to a future president, Eleanor Roosevelt was given away by another president—her uncle Teddy Roosevelt. Eleanor was Franklin's partner in the presidency, attending political meetings, speaking out on issues, and writing a daily newspaper column. No president's wife had done those things before. Eleanor Roosevelt is one of the most admired first ladies of all time. She is remembered for helping the poor, for her war efforts, and for her work with the United Nations.

"If I am asked whether the American people will pull themselves out of this depression, I answer, 'They will if they want to.'" Franklin Roosevelt often gave speeches on the radio. He called these speeches "fireside chats." In these informal talks, it seemed as if the president were speaking directly to each American. Roosevelt explained to people what he was trying to do and often outlined what they could do to help. The president's smooth voice reassured the worried Americans.

When Roosevelt ran for president in 1932, the nation was suffering from the Great Depression. After he was elected, Roosevelt brought people hope and helped restore their faith in the country. He told Americans, "the only thing we have to fear is fear itself." Roosevelt solved the economic problems with a program called the New Deal, which created jobs and helped regulate the banking industry.

Roosevelt was reelected for a second term in 1936 and for a third term in 1940. By then, World War II was raging in other parts of the world. In 1941, the United States entered the war when the Japanese bombed Pearl Harbor. With the war still on in 1944, Roosevelt was elected for a fourth term. Roosevelt worked with other world leaders to end the war. When Roosevelt died in office, the nation was deeply saddened. Within months of Roosevelt's death, the war ended.

Roosevelt is the only president to be elected to four terms. In 1951, Congress passed the Twenty-second Amendment, which limits presidents to two terms. Shown are some campaign buttons for Roosevelt, along with some anti-Roosevelt buttons.

HARRY S. TRUMAN

When Truman became president after Roosevelt's death, he told reporters, "I felt like the moon, the stars, and all the planets had fallen on me." Most historians agree that Truman rose to the mighty tasks put before him when he became president.

Truman grew up in Missouri. His parents gave him the middle name "S" to stand for both their fathers' names, which began with that initial. He didn't go to college but worked instead on his family farm. He served in France during World War I and returned to marry his childhood sweetheart. A few years later, Truman decided to go into politics, eventually becoming a U.S. senator. In 1944, he was President Roosevelt's running mate, and he became vice-president. After Roosevelt's sudden death five weeks into the term, Truman became president.

Having been president for only one month, Truman made one of the most important decisions in world history. He tried desperately to get the Japanese to surrender and end World War II. When they didn't, Truman decided to use a "secret weapon," the atomic bomb, to try to bring a swift end to the war. Soon after these devastating attacks, the Japanese surrendered.

33rd President
Born: May 8, 1884
Died: December 26, 1972

Term of Office
1945 to 1953

Party
Democratic

Vice-president
1st term: none
2nd term: Alben William Barkley

First Lady
Elizabeth (Bess) Virginia Wallace Truman

Truman worked hard during his reelection campaign, traveling across the country to make more than 350 speeches. Some people didn't expect Truman to win. One newspaper printed its headline before the results were actually in. Truman was delighted to show off the incorrect newspaper.

Truman was known as a family man, devoted to his wife, Bess, and daughter, Margaret. They were sometimes called "The Three Musketeers." When Margaret didn't receive a good review for her singing concert, President Truman sent an angry letter to the critic, showing that he was a proud papa.

72

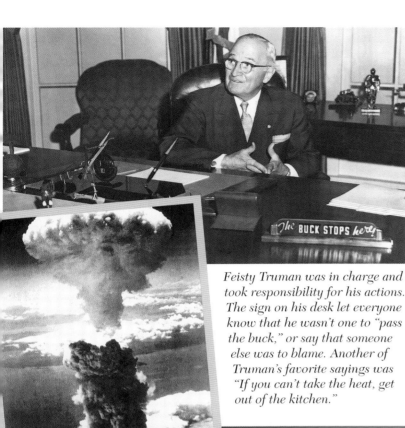

After the war, Truman focused on giving all Americans a "Fair Deal" on jobs and housing. In 1948, he was reelected. Events overseas showed Truman's effective leadership skills. The Soviet Union wanted many countries to follow their system of rule, communism. The United States did not approve of this system and vowed to help any countries fighting to stay free. This was called the Truman Doctrine. In 1950, Truman sent aid when communist North Korea attacked South Korea. When a similar problem arose in Vietnam, Truman sent help there, too.

Truman decided not to seek office again, and he retired to Missouri in 1953. Truman died almost 20 years later.

Feisty Truman was in charge and took responsibility for his actions. The sign on his desk let everyone know that he wasn't one to "pass the buck," or say that someone else was to blame. Another of Truman's favorite sayings was "If you can't take the heat, get out of the kitchen."

With World War II drawing to a close, Truman sent a message to the Japanese: "The alternative to surrender is prompt and utter destruction." The Japanese did not surrender. Truman then ordered an atomic bomb to be dropped on Japan. On August 6, 1945, a B-29 bomber named the Enola Gay dropped a bomb on Hiroshima. Many thousands of people died instantly. Still more died later from injuries. Days later, another atomic bomb was dropped on the city of Nagasaki.

At the end of World War II, Truman helped create the United Nations. This organization was set up to help prevent wars, to help protect people's rights, and also to aid the economies of countries around the world. It is made up of representatives from many nations.

After World War II, the "Cold War" began. The Soviet Union wanted to spread its influence around the world, and the United States vowed to help keep nations free. In 1948, the Soviets stopped Berlin, a city in Germany, from getting supplies. But the United States and Great Britain dropped food, coal, and more from planes. In part because of the Berlin airlift, Truman formed a group called NATO (North Atlantic Treaty Organization), which united Western Europe, Canada, and the United States.

DWIGHT D. EISENHOWER

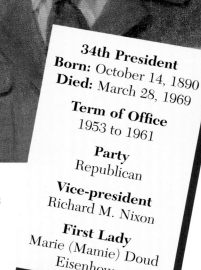

Like several presidents before him, Eisenhower won the office because of his popularity as a war hero. Eisenhower was so popular, in fact, that both parties wanted him as a candidate. People remember the Eisenhower years for the peace he worked to uphold in our country and overseas.

Dwight David Eisenhower grew up with five brothers in Kansas. He attended the U.S. Military Academy at West Point and began a career in the Army. He asked for active duty in World War I, but he was assigned to train others to fight instead. In World War II, however, his strong leadership skills were recognized. He led troops into North Africa and Italy. President Roosevelt promoted him to the highest position—supreme commander of all Allied forces. Eisenhower's strategies helped win the war.

After the war, people tried to get Ike, as he was known, to run for president. He refused. Then, in 1952, he was convinced to run for president and won. As president, Eisenhower focused on peace. As a

34th President
Born: October 14, 1890
Died: March 28, 1969

Term of Office
1953 to 1961

Party
Republican

Vice-president
Richard M. Nixon

First Lady
Marie (Mamie) Doud Eisenhower

When Eisenhower became president there were separate schools for black children and white children. In a landmark case, the U.S. Supreme Court voted that children of all races should attend school together. People in Little Rock, Arkansas, threatened to disobey this rule in 1957. They tried to prevent nine black students from attending an all-white high school. Eisenhower sent in federal troops to assist the "Little Rock Nine," as they were known.

During Eisenhower's presidency, Alaska and Hawaii became states. The states then numbered 50, as they still do today.

soldier, he said, he had seen too much war. Following the election, Eisenhower went to Korea, where the North and the South of the country were at war. Peace came a few months later because of his efforts.

Americans were shocked and unhappy that the Soviet Union launched the first satellite into outer space. Called Sputnik, meaning "fellow traveler," it was the first human-made object to orbit the earth. America vowed to get ahead in the space race.

Americans felt at ease with Eisenhower running the country. In 1956, he won a second term by a huge majority. One of his goals was equal rights for all Americans. "There must be no second class citizens in this country," he wrote.

When he left the White House after his second term, Eisenhower moved with his wife to a farm near Gettysburg, Pennsylvania. Eisenhower died ten years later.

When Eisenhower played golf during his presidency, many people took up the sport. Eisenhower liked golf so much that he had a putting green put in on the White House lawn. Eisenhower also enjoyed painting and was quite a good cook.

Because of Eisenhower's career in the military, the Eisenhower family moved often—28 times, in fact. The eight years they spent in the White House were the most they had lived in any one place. Eisenhower and his wife later retired to a farm in Pennsylvania, which was the first house they ever owned.

People found it easy to like Eisenhower. They remembered his courageous wartime service. He had an easy way about him, and he always seemed to be smiling. People of both parties wore buttons with "I Like Ike" on them, and many women carried nail files or makeup cases with those words. With women making up half of voters, Republicans gave away women's items printed with their candidate's slogan.

Eisenhower tried to improve relations with the Soviet Union, but neither side could trust the other. Eisenhower believed the "domino theory," the idea that the Soviets' ruling method, communism, could spread from one country to the next like a row of falling dominoes.

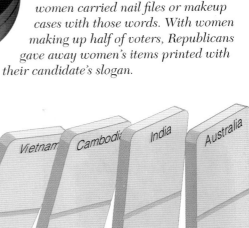

JOHN F. KENNEDY

Although John F. Kennedy spent only about 1,000 days as president, he had a long-lasting effect on the nation. His ideals for peace, equality, and service to the nation inspired many Americans. At age 43, he was the youngest man ever elected president. He was also the youngest president to die in office.

John Fitzgerald Kennedy was born into a large, wealthy family in Boston. Handsome and outgoing, he attended Harvard University and then joined the Navy during World War II. After showing extreme courage in the war, Kennedy returned home a hero and went into politics. He became a U.S. congressman and then a U.S. senator. In 1960, he ran for president and won by a very narrow margin.

Kennedy was an idealist—someone who believes the best can happen. He wanted Americans to work together to help all people. Kennedy challenged citizens to "ask not what your country can do for you—ask what you can do for your country."

Kennedy showed his bravery again when the country faced grave danger in October 1962.

35th President
Born: May 29, 1917
Died: November 22, 1963

Term of Office
1961 to 1963

Party
Democratic

Vice-president
Lyndon B. Johnson

First Lady
Jacqueline Bouvier Kennedy

President Kennedy created the Peace Corps so that Americans could help people outside the United States. Many people, some just out of college, traveled to other countries and volunteered to help people improve their living conditions. The Peace Corps helped many nations build hospitals, set up schools, and learn better farming practices.

Kennedy vowed to win the space race with the Soviet Union. In office only a short time, he promised to land a man on the moon before the decade was out. It seemed that the Soviets were winning the race when they put Yuri Gagarin in orbit around the planet. A few weeks later, the United States launched Alan Shepard into space. The United States landed a man on the moon in 1969.

The Soviet Union was sending nuclear missiles to Cuba, just 90 miles away from American soil. Acting swiftly, Kennedy sent Navy ships to surround Cuba and stop the Soviet Union from sending in more weapons. On the edge of nuclear war, the Soviets withdrew from Cuba.

In World War II, Kennedy was the skipper of a small patrol torpedo, or PT boat, that was sunk when it was rammed by a Japanese warship. Although badly hurt by the crash, Kennedy saved the surviving crew members. He swam for several hours, towing another man to safety by clenching the man's life-jacket strap in his teeth. Kennedy won a medal for his bravery.

On November 22, 1963, Kennedy went to make a speech in Dallas, Texas. People cheered his arrival. He rode through the streets in an open car, sitting next to his wife, Jacqueline. Shots rang out, and Kennedy was killed by an assassin. The shocked nation mourned their lively young president and grieved with his family. The reason for the assassination and who was responsible remain something of a mystery today.

Almost every American alive in 1963 remembers exactly what they were doing when they found out that Kennedy had been killed. During Kennedy's funeral, a riderless horse represented the country's loss. The nation wept as three-year-old John-John saluted when his father's casket passed by.

The Kennedys were a popular first family. First Lady Jacqueline Kennedy's great sense of style prompted many women to try to copy the "Jackie Look." The Kennedy children, Caroline and John, Jr. (sometimes called John-John), captured the nation's heart. John sometimes hid under his father's desk in the Oval Office.

LYNDON BAINES JOHNSON

L yndon Johnson wanted what he called the "Great Society" for America. He worked to bring equality to all people and to improve conditions for the poor. Johnson was able to make many Americans' lives better, but, at the same time, the country became deeply divided over the war in Vietnam.

Lyndon Baines Johnson was born in the Texas Hill Country. Johnson's grandfather and father had served in the state legislature, but the family struggled along with very little money. After attending college in Texas, Johnson taught school in South Texas. His students were poor, and Johnson saw what that kind of life was really like.

Johnson went to work for a U.S. congressman, and then he ran for office himself. He served in the House of Representatives for six straight terms. He took leave from Congress to fight in the Navy in World War II, and he won a Silver Star. In 1948, he won a seat in the U.S. Senate and was reelected the following term.

In 1960, Johnson became Kennedy's vice-president. After Kennedy's assassination, Johnson took over as president. In 1964, Johnson won the

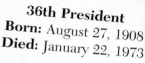

36th President
Born: August 27, 1908
Died: January 22, 1973

Term of Office
1963 to 1969

Party
Democratic

Vice-president
1st term: none
2nd term: Hubert Humphrey

First Lady
Claudia (Lady Bird) Taylor Johnson

Johnson's pets were very important to him and were popular with the country, too. The pair of beagles he brought with him to the White House, Him and Her, appeared on a magazine cover.

Johnson loved vehicles. Visitors to his Texas ranch were often treated to tours in his Lincoln Continental—at high speeds. Johnson liked to play tricks on visitors with another vehicle. He would drive down a hill near the river and pretend that the brakes were going out. The car would plunge into the water, but to the visitors' surprise, it floated. It was an Amphicar, a special kind of car that runs both on the road and in the water.

Both President and Mrs. Johnson cared a great deal about the environment. President Johnson worked to get laws passed to stop pollution of rivers and the air. Mrs. Johnson worked to limit billboards on highways. She also encouraged people to landscape with plants that grow naturally in their areas. Today, the Lady Bird Johnson National Wildflower Research Center continues their work.

As Air Force One *flew back to Washington, D.C., after Kennedy's assassination, Johnson took the oath of office as president. Judge Sarah Hughes of Dallas conducted the ceremony, making Johnson the first president ever sworn in by a woman. A few days after Kennedy's funeral, Johnson said, "No words are sad enough to express our sense of loss. No words are strong enough to express our determination to continue the forward thrust of America that he began."*

presidency in his own right, with the widest margin of popular votes in American history.

Johnson declared a "war on poverty," and he started programs to improve city slums and other poor areas. He got Congress to pass laws to help older people pay their medical bills. He also encouraged Congress to pass laws that made sure all people had equal rights in voting, education, and more. But the war in Vietnam cast a shadow over Johnson's good works. Many people thought that the United States should stay out of the conflict between North and South Vietnam, but Johnson sent troops to help South Vietnam. People grew unhappy with Johnson. Knowing this, he did not run again. Johnson retired to his Texas ranch and died a few years later.

ALL THE
WAY WITH
LBJ

During Johnson's presidency, the LBJ Ranch House (above) became known as "The Texas White House." Johnson said, "All the world is welcome here." Preferring his home turf, Johnson often conducted state business in the front yard of his ranch house with important men seated around him in lawn chairs. Johnson was a powerful communicator, and he was known for his ability to get people to do things he wanted done. Also pictured is the house in which Johnson was born.

RICHARD M. NIXON

Richard Milhous Nixon is the only president to resign from office. He left the White House after the public found out about his misuse of the powers of the presidency. But Nixon accomplished some important things during his terms, especially in building relations with other countries.

Nixon was born in California, where he helped his struggling family run a grocery store. He excelled in college in California and later at Duke University Law School. Nixon returned home to practice law. After fighting in World War II, he was elected to the House of Representatives and later to the Senate. Eisenhower chose Nixon as his running mate in 1952. After serving as vice-president, Nixon's party nominated him for president in 1960. Nixon barely lost to John F. Kennedy. Nixon went back to California, ran for governor, and again lost. After that, Nixon seemed to be done with politics. Then Nixon made quite a comeback. In 1968, he was again nominated for president, and this time he won.

In the White House, Nixon set out to further world peace. He called his plan "détente," which means to relax strained relations. Nixon greatly improved U.S. relations with China and the Soviet Union. He helped bring about a treaty to limit nuclear weapons. These successes helped Nixon win reelection in 1972, but he would not complete this term. The public learned that during the campaign, Nixon's associates broke into the Democratic Party offices at the Watergate building in Washington, D.C. They were hoping to find information to use in the campaign. At first, Nixon denied knowing anything about the break-in, but it was later proved that he did know. Nixon faced impeachment, but instead he resigned on August 9, 1974. He retired with his wife near New York City. Over the next 20 years, he wrote books about his public life.

37th President
Born: January 9, 1913
Died: April 22, 1994

Term of Office
1969 to 1974

Party
Republican

Vice-presidents
1st term, part of 2nd term: Spiro T. Agnew
2nd term end: Gerald R. Ford

First Lady
Thelma Catherine (Pat) Ryan Nixon

Nixon and Agnew won the 1972 campaign by a landslide—their opponents had more votes in only one state. About a year and a half later, neither Nixon nor Agnew would be in office. Agnew was replaced by Gerald Ford. When Nixon resigned, Vice-president Ford became president.

Nixon was the first president to visit China. He made history again a few months later by visiting the Soviet Union. These remarkable trips helped ease strained relations between the nations.

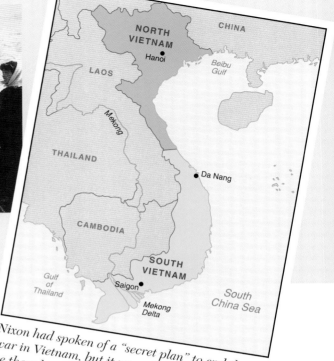

Nixon was a deeply devoted family man. His daughter Tricia was married during Nixon's first term in the White House. Nixon's other daughter, Julie, married one of Dwight Eisenhower's grandsons.

Nixon had spoken of a "secret plan" to end the war in Vietnam, but it proved more difficult than he thought. Nixon ordered more bombing of North Vietnam, and in 1973, he withdrew U.S. troops. Many Americans were displeased with the outcome—many lives were lost, much money was spent, and North Vietnam took control of South Vietnam just two years after the peace announcement.

Rock star Elvis Presley asked to meet with President Nixon because he was concerned about the country. Presley dropped off a handwritten letter at the White House gate. Later, the famous meeting between Nixon and Elvis took place in the White House.

One of the most exciting events in American history happened during Nixon's first term. On July 29, 1969, American astronauts landed on the moon. Upon leaving the first footprints in space, Neil Armstrong said, "That's one small step for a man, one giant leap for mankind." From the White House, Nixon spoke to the astronauts on the moon.

GERALD R. FORD

Gerald R. Ford became president in a unique way—he was neither elected president nor vice-president. Instead, Ford became commander in chief because of scandal. First, Richard Nixon appointed him vice-president when Spiro T. Agnew resigned. Then Nixon was forced to resign, and Ford found himself president. Ford worked to restore honor to the White House.

Ford was born in Nebraska and raised in Michigan. He was a star athlete in high school and at the University of Michigan. He graduated from Yale Law School. During World War II, Ford earned ten battle stars. After the war, he practiced law in Michigan and entered politics. He served in Congress for more than 25 years. He was known for his charm, easy manner, and willingness to work with people whose views differed from his. When Nixon had to replace Agnew, he looked to Ford. He knew that Ford was an honest, well-respected man. Ford served as vice-president for

38th President
Born: July 14, 1913
Died: December 26, 2006

Term of Office
1974 to 1977

Party
Republican

Vice-president
Nelson Aldrich Rockefeller

First Lady
Elizabeth (Betty) Bloomer Warren Ford

When Ford pardoned Nixon, many people thought a secret deal had been made between the two men. But Ford said, "I am indebted to no man and only one woman—my dear wife...." Betty Ford was an outspoken first lady. She worked for women's rights and women's health issues.

Gerald Ford could have played professional football for either the Detroit Lions or Green Bay Packers, but he turned them down. Instead, he worked as a boxing coach and assistant football coach at Yale. He coached full-time while attending Yale Law School.

Ford tried to rally the country's economy with a campaign called "Whip Inflation Now." People wore the buttons to show that they wanted to stop rising prices.

nine months. During that time, Nixon was involved in the Watergate scandal. (During Nixon's reelection campaign, some Nixon workers broke into the opponents' headquarters. They hoped to get information to hurt their opponents' images.) When Nixon faced impeachment, he resigned. Ford became president and took the oath of office.

As president, Ford set to work to heal the country. "The long national nightmare is over," he stated. "Our Constitution works." Just a month after taking office, Ford granted Nixon a pardon, meaning that Nixon would not be tried for any crimes. Ford thought this was the best way for the country to move forward, but many people were unhappy about the pardon.

During his term, Ford tried to build the economy and worked to maintain U.S. power overseas. He ran for president in 1976, but he did not win. He retired to California and died at age 93, the longest-lived president in U.S. history.

The year 1975 was very dramatic for Ford. He ordered U.S. forces to rescue an American ship, the U.S.S. Mayaguez, which had been seized by Cambodian gunboats. The ship was returned with its crew of 39, but 41 Americans lost their lives in the mission. Also in 1975, on two different trips to California, Ford was the target of assassination attempts.

During Ford's term, the country celebrated its bicentennial, or 200th birthday. The Queen of England visited to mark the celebration. There was more dancing in the White House during Ford's term—his daughter, Susan, held her high school prom there.

JIMMY CARTER

When James Earl Carter, Jr., entered the White House, he was set on changing the way that government worked. He had an informal style that appealed to many Americans. As president, Jimmy, as he liked to be called, faced troubled economic times and challenges to America's power from overseas.

Carter grew up near tiny Plains, Georgia, where his family farm, politics, and the Baptist church were important to him. An excellent student who wanted to see the world, Carter entered the U.S. Naval Academy. He served as a Navy officer until his father died. Carter then went home to run the family farm. The farm did well, and Carter got into state politics, becoming a state senator and then governor of Georgia. In 1976, he ran for president, although few people outside of Georgia had ever heard of him. Carter won by a slight margin.

39th President
Born: October 1, 1924
Term of Office
1977 to 1981
Party
Democratic
Vice-president
Walter Frederick Mondale
First Lady
Rosalynn Smith Carter

When the Panama Canal was built in 1914, the United States leased the land and took control of the canal, and the U.S. flag few over the canal. President Carter arranged for the ownership of the canal to be transferred to Panama. Although Latin Americans were happy about this, many Americans were not. Now the flag of Panama is flown at the canal.

Carter had a casual, down-home style. Although many presidents rode in fancy cars during their inaugural parades, Carter walked with his family. When traveling as president, Carter often carried his own luggage and stayed in people's homes instead of hotels. He often wore sweaters instead of suits. Carter had a tree house built on the White House lawn for his nine-year-old daughter, Amy.

In 1979, a serious accident occurred at a nuclear power plant near Harrisburg, Pennsylvania. Carter and his wife, Rosalynn, flew to the site to reassure the American people. Carter had long been interested in nuclear power. At the Naval Academy, Carter worked on the first nuclear submarine.

Carter invited Egyptian President Anwar Sadat and Israeli Prime Minister Menachem Begin to the presidential retreat in Maryland. There had long been fighting and violence between Israel and Egypt. Carter played a leading role in getting the governments to agree on a peace treaty.

As president, Carter worked to provide more jobs and bring prices down. The economy stayed in trouble, though. Carter had a difficult time working with Congress. Things were difficult overseas, too. Carter was concerned about human rights all over the world. He helped work out an important peace agreement between Egypt and Israel through the Camp David Accords. But a situation in Iran prompted serious trouble. A group of 52 Americans working for the U.S. government were taken hostage. Carter sent a rescue team, but the mission failed.

Carter did not win a second term. The day he left the White House, the hostages were released. Carter retired to Georgia. He continues to work for world peace and human rights. He is involved in many projects to help the needy.

Carter and his wife, Rosalynn, have been busy in retirement. They led a team to observe the June 1999 elections in Indonesia, the country's first free elections since 1955. They also volunteer with Habitat for Humanity.

When the Soviet Union invaded the country of Afghanistan, Carter led more than 60 nations in a boycott of the 1980 summer Olympics. He also cut off all grain sales to the Soviet Union. The United States and the Soviets had been discussing more limitations to nuclear arms, but the treaty was not approved by Congress.

RONALD REAGAN

President Ronald Reagan once said, "What I'd really like to do is go down in history as the president who made Americans believe in themselves again." His term in the White House went a long way toward that goal. As the oldest president ever elected (at age 69), Reagan focused on several key issues, such as making government smaller and improving relations with the Soviet Union. Reagan accomplished much, but some of his solutions created more problems, such as a large national debt.

Reagan grew up in small towns in Illinois. An outgoing and handsome boy, he attended a small Illinois college. After graduation, Reagan worked as a sportscaster in radio. Then he went to Hollywood and hosted two popular television shows and appeared in movies.

While an actor, Reagan got involved in politics. In 1966, he became governor of California and then served another term. In 1980, Reagan ran for president and defeated Jimmy Carter. In office, Reagan wanted to improve the economy. He cut taxes and lowered some government spending. But he increased military spending to defend against the "evil empire," as he called the Soviet Union. Reagan held talks with Soviet leader Mikhail Gorbachev, and relations between the two nations improved. There were problems with other nations, though. Some Americans had been kidnapped in Beirut, Lebanon. Although Reagan said that the United States would not bargain for their release, the nation learned that some U.S. officials had sold guns to Iran in trade for the hostages. Reagan was not directly involved, but some of his staff resigned because of the scandal.

After two terms, Reagan retired to California. The popular president was diagnosed with Alzheimer's disease, an illness that affects memory. Nevertheless, he lived to be 93.

40th President
Born: February 6, 1911
Died: June 5, 2004

Term of Office
1981 to 1989

Party
Republican

Vice-president
George H. W. Bush

First Lady
Nancy Davis Reagan

The Reagans spent time at their California ranch, Rancho del Cielo, or "Ranch in the Sky." President Reagan often cared for the horses and enjoyed trail rides.

Reagan knew how to handle the media. To keep some interviews with the press short, Reagan would take questions from reporters with his helicopter thundering in the background.

Nancy Reagan was often criticized as first lady. Some people felt she had too much influence on the president and spent too much money redecorating the White House. She is remembered positively for her efforts in the war against drugs and her "Just Say No" campaign.

Reagan is the only president who was once a movie actor. Reagan appeared in over 50 films. During World War II, Reagan's war effort involved movies—he made training films. In one movie, Bedtime for Bonzo, Reagan even acted with a chimpanzee. Nancy Reagan also acted in Hollywood before she became first lady. The two starred together in one film about World War II.

Because of his experience in television and film, Reagan was a skilled speaker. People called Reagan "The Great Communicator," and many credit his speaking ability for much of his success. He inspired the nation with sayings such as, "America is too great for small dreams."

Reagan had a big impact on the courts during his presidency. He appointed many federal judges and three Supreme Court judges. Reagan's appointment of Sandra Day O'Connor added the first woman to the country's highest court.

Reagan led the country through some difficult times. Just a few months after he was elected, Reagan was shot, but he recovered fairly quickly. In 1983, terrorists bombed a U.S. building in Beirut. In 1986, the space shuttle Challenger exploded and the crew was killed.

GEORGE H. W. BUSH

George Herbert Walker Bush followed his eight years as vice-president to Ronald Reagan with a term as president. In the White House, Bush tried to make the United States, in his words, "a kinder, gentler nation."

Bush grew up on the East Coast and went to the best private schools. A man of duty, he spent his eighteenth birthday enlisting in the Navy. As a World War II pilot, he flew dangerous missions and earned awards for his bravery. After the war, he graduated from Yale with honors. He moved to West Texas to work in the oil business.

In Texas, Bush entered politics. He served two terms in the U.S. House of Representatives and ran twice for the Senate, but he was defeated. He was then appointed to important posts, such as the U.S. ambassador to the United Nations and director of the Central Intelligence Agency. In 1980, Bush ran for vice-president on Ronald Reagan's ticket

41st President
Born: June 12, 1924

Term of Office
1989 to 1993

Party
Republican

Vice-president
James Danforth (Dan) Quayle

First Lady
Barbara Pierce Bush

In 1990, the president's dog, Millie, "wrote" a book. In reality, Mrs. Bush wrote the book from the dog's point of view. The book told about a day in the life of a White House dog. Many people loved Millie's Book, making it a best seller.

GEORGE HERBERT WALKER BUSH
Service Branch:
USN
Rank / Rate:
LT
Service Dates:
1942 to 1945
Born:
MILTON, MA
06/12/24
Photo: USS SAN JACINTO

Bush was the youngest Navy pilot during World War II. He named his bomber after his sweetheart, Barbara. On one bombing mission, Bush's plane was shot down by the Japanese. He was rescued by the crew of a U.S. submarine. Bush earned the Distinguished Flying Cross for his courage.

Active in retirement, Bush made a parachute jump similar to the one he made during World War II.

George Bush served as captain of the Yale baseball team. Here he is receiving a gift from legendary baseball player Babe Ruth. Ruth is handing over the book he wrote about his life for display at the Yale library.

Barbara Bush was a popular first lady. She devoted herself to the cause of helping adults who did not know how to read. The Bushes had four sons and two daughters— one daughter died in childhood. Two sons, George and Jeb, followed the family tradition of politics. Their grandfather was a senator.

and won. In 1988, when Bush won the presidency, he wanted to steady the nation with traditional American values.

As president, Bush saw the Soviet Union collapse and communism around the world decline. But new challenges were ahead. In 1989, Bush sent U.S military forces to Panama to bring its leader, Manuel Noriega, to stand trial on drug charges. A year later, when the country of Iraq invaded its neighbor, Kuwait, Bush again sent troops to fight.

The United States saw a swift victory in the Persian Gulf War. At home, there were more challenges. Bush had pledged not to raise taxes, but he needed to reduce the national debt. In the next election, voters were unhappy with Bush and elected Bill Clinton instead. Bush retired to Texas and became the second president to have a son follow him to the White House.

The environment was a big issue during Bush's term. The Exxon Valdez, a large ship carrying oil, had crashed and spilled oil off the coast of Alaska. The pollution seriously harmed the environment, and people around the world grew concerned. In 1992, many nations met to discuss how they could work together to take care of the earth.

After World War II, Germany was divided by the Berlin Wall. One side was communist and the other was not. In 1990, the wall was broken down (shown near left). This signaled an end to the Cold War.

WILLIAM JEFFERSON CLINTON

With William Jefferson Clinton in the White House, the United States enjoyed an era of peace and economic good times. Clinton's record is balanced with a personal scandal that led to his impeachment and trial for crimes committed while in office.

Clinton was actually born William Jefferson Blythe IV, but his father died a few months before he was born. Clinton's mother remarried, and he eventually took on the family name Clinton. Clinton grew up in Arkansas, where he excelled in school and took an interest in politics. Clinton graduated from Georgetown University and won a Rhodes Scholarship to Oxford University in England. After getting a law degree from Yale, Clinton entered politics.

Clinton served first as Arkansas's attorney general and then as governor in 1978. He lost reelection but tried again four years later and won. Because he wouldn't give up, Clinton earned the nickname "The Comeback Kid." Clinton was governor until he won the 1992 presidential race.

42nd President
Born: August 19, 1946

Term of Office
1993 to 2001

Party
Democratic

Vice-president
Albert Gore, Jr.

First Lady
Hillary Rodham Clinton

Clinton once thought about a career in music. During the 1992 campaign, Clinton shared his talent and his fun-loving side with the public by playing his saxophone on national television.

Clinton believed in a politician's power to change people's lives. "There is nothing wrong with America that cannot be cured by what is right with America," he said. He pushed through laws to help working Americans and to protect citizens from gun violence, including the Brady Bill. Sara and James Brady are pictured at right.

In high school, Clinton met President John F. Kennedy. After a handshake in the White House Rose Garden, Clinton decided to seek a life in public service.

90

Hillary Clinton played an active role in her husband's presidency. She was so active, in fact, that some people felt she had too much power. Mrs. Clinton worked for causes she believed in, such as changes to the health-care system and children's rights. The Clintons have one daughter, Chelsea. One day at school, Chelsea suggested that school officials call her father, the president, to see whether she could take some medicine. Her mother, Chelsea said, was too busy to take the call.

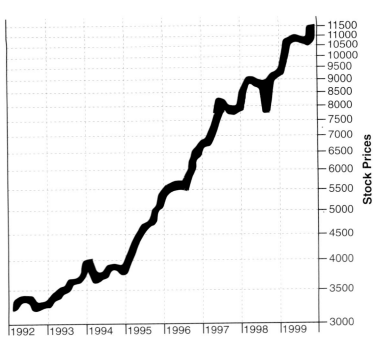

Under Clinton, the U.S. economy boomed. Stock prices rose. (Stocks are individually owned shares of a company.) Most people had jobs. For the first time since the late 1960s, the government was spending less money than it was taking in.

During the impeachment process, the country was divided in its views about Clinton. Some felt he had seriously hurt the office of president. Others believed Clinton's private life should be private. Clinton apologized to the nation for his actions.

As president, Clinton worked with his wife, Hillary, to change the way the American health-care system works. But their plan was not accepted. Clinton then focused on managing the budget and taxes. He also worked to create trade agreements with other countries. With an eye on the world, Clinton tried to end fighting in the Middle East, Europe, and other parts of the globe. America was doing well, and Clinton was reelected.

Throughout his presidency, Clinton had been accused of breaking laws. Because he lied about a matter in his personal life, he became the second president ever to be impeached and tried by Congress. Clinton was not removed from office, though. At the end of his second term, Clinton moved to New York State, where his wife had been elected a U.S. senator.

In the former Yugoslavia, several groups were fighting a terrible war. President Clinton brought leaders together and helped them agree on a plan for peace. As part of the plan, Clinton sent U.S. troops on a peace-keeping mission to the country of Bosnia. Clinton defended human rights in other parts of the world, too.

91

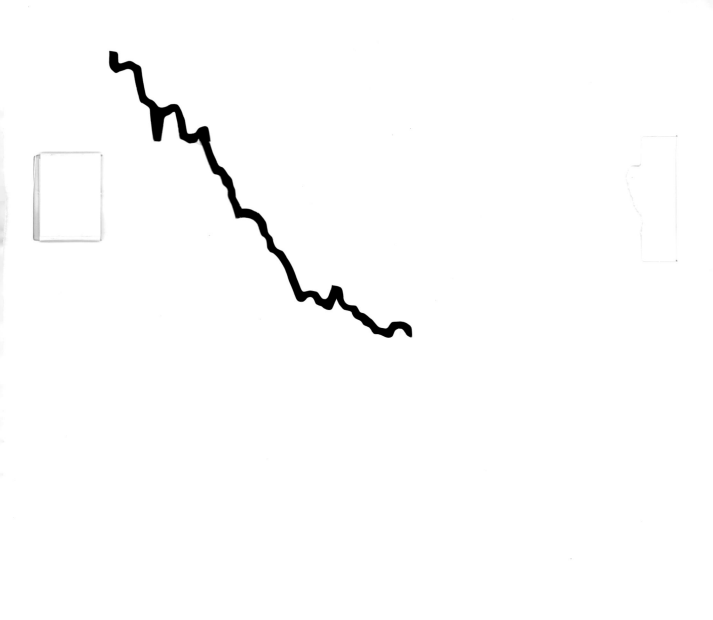

GEORGE W. BUSH

The historic election of 2000 ended with George W. Bush winning the presidency by five electoral votes. Bush's victory marked the first time since 1888 that a man who did not win the popular vote won the White House. Bush is only the second president ever to have a father who held the office before him.

Bush grew up in Texas, as part of a family with traditions in politics. He attended college on the East Coast, earning a degree from Yale and a master's degree from Harvard. During the Vietnam War, he served in the Texas Air Guard as a pilot.

By 1975, Bush was back in Texas trying his hand in the oil and gas industry, but he found it a struggle. In 1988, he worked on his father's presidential campaign, helping him gain the office. A lifelong baseball fan, Bush and a group of partners bought the Texas Rangers baseball team in 1989. Bush

43rd President
Born: July 6, 1946

Term of Office
2001 to 2009

Party
Republican

Vice-president
Richard Bruce Cheney

First Lady
Laura Welch Bush

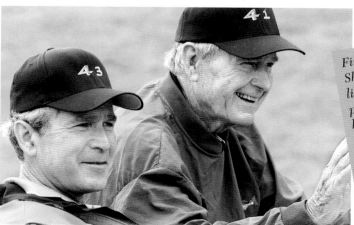

President Bush and his father were known to joke around by greeting each other as "Mr. President." The elder Bush sometimes teased the younger one by calling him "Quincy," after John Quincy Adams—the first man to follow his father to the White House. The Bushes are shown here wearing caps that mark the number of each one's presidency.

First Lady Laura Bush also grew up in Texas. She is a former public school teacher and librarian. Mrs. Bush worked on programs to promote reading and education. The Bushes have twin daughters—Barbara and Jenna—who are named after their grandmothers.

was involved with the team until he took up the political torch—he was elected governor of Texas in 1994. As governor, Bush used his wit and humor to cross political party lines. In 1998, Bush was reelected in a landslide victory.

In 2000, Bush entered the presidential race against Vice-president Al Gore. The race was close throughout but never closer than on election night. The results were not confirmed for more than five weeks. Then, it took a Supreme Court decision to decide the race. In his second election President Bush won more handily. He focused on national security, lowering taxes, and improving public schools.

Bush takes his first oath of office. Knowing that some people believe the outcome of the race was unfair, Bush pledged to work with both political parties and asked for his opponents' support. Bush kept promises to include Americans from diverse backgrounds in important government jobs.

Never before had a presidential race been decided by the Supreme Court. The outcome of the race raised questions about the election process. People debate whether the electoral college is an old idea that should be done away with.

When planes crashed into U.S. landmarks on September 11, 2001, President Bush helped Americans rally together. The leadership he showed during this time was a defining moment of his presidency.

As a child, Bush wanted to be a baseball star like his idol, Willie Mays. Although not an expert player, Bush is a dedicated fan of the game and once was part-owner of the Texas Rangers major league baseball team. So when he got to the White House, it was "take me out to the T-ball game." Bush invited Little League teams to play ball on the White House lawn.

BARACK OBAMA

On November 4, 2008, President-elect Barack Obama told a crowd of supporters, "Change has come to America. This is your victory."

One change he spoke of was especially significant. It was the first time an African American had been elected president.

Obama grew up mostly in Hawaii, raised by a single mother with help from his grandparents. His father was from Kenya, Africa, and returned there to live when Obama was very young.

Obama's family didn't have much money, but he went to Columbia University by getting scholarships and loans. He went on to law school at Harvard. After law school, Obama returned to Chicago in 1991. He became active in the community by helping people register to vote. While in the Senate, Obama worked to pass laws to cut taxes for working families and to improve health care. In 2004 he ran for a seat in the United States Senate and was elected by a huge majority of the voters in Illinois.

44th President
Born: August 4, 1961

Term of Office
2009 to present

Party
Democratic

Vice-president
Joseph Robinette Biden, Jr.

First Lady
Michelle Robinson Obama

Obama entered the 2008 race for the presidency against Republican candidate John McCain. Obama brought a message of hope and change to American voters. Many people believed deeply in this message and cast their vote for him.

Obama became president at a time of great challenge for America. Among his first challenges as president were ending the wars in Iraq and Afghanistan, helping many families in the United States solve their money problems, and making sure people had jobs. Seeing these problems, on the night he was elected Obama said, "The road ahead will be long. Our climb will be steep . . . but America, I've never been more hopeful than I am tonight that we will get there."

Michelle Obama planted a vegetable garden on the White House lawn. One of her goals is to get children to eat healthful foods that are grown locally. By growing foods that will be served at the White House, the first lady hopes to encourage others to grow some of their own food.

First Lady Michelle Obama is also a lawyer, but she has said that her most important job is that of mom to daughters Malia and Sasha. The Obama girls are the first young children to live in the White House in many years. This First Family will not only host important state dinners for world leaders, but also will hold fun-filled sleepovers for their young daughters and friends.

During the inauguration, emotions ran high. Many people were crying, hugging, and cheering. President Obama described challenges for the country. He expressed his belief in the nation, saying "All this we can do. All this we will do." At one point, the crowd broke into the famous chant, "Yes, we can!"

In the past, presidential campaigns often used radio and television, but Obama spread his message on the Internet by using YouTube videos. They were viewed by millions of people.

Less than 50 years ago, African Americans were fighting for equal rights. Today, after Obama's historic victory, an African American holds the country's highest office.

The National Education Association paired with a Web site called kidthing.com to ask young people around the world to write letters to President Obama. More than 4,500 letters poured in, sharing childrens' hopes and dreams for the country.

INDEX

Caption citations are listed in italics.